Accidentally
OVERWEIGHT

Solve Your Weight Loss Puzzle

Dr Libby Weaver

Disclaimer

The contents of this book are for information only and are intended to assist readers in identifying symptoms and conditions they may be experiencing. This book is not intended to be a substitute for obtaining proper medical advice and must not be relied upon in this way. Always consult a qualified doctor or health practitioner. The author and publisher do not accept responsibility for illness arising out of the failure to seek medical advice from a doctor. In the event that you use any of the information in this book for yourself or your family or friends, the author and the publisher assume no responsibility for your actions.

First published in the USA in 2011

Published by Little Green Frog Publishing Ltd
www.littlegreenfrogpublishing.com

ISBN: 978-0-473-18148-2

For Christopher
with spectacular gratitude

Table of Contents

Guidelines for Getting the Most out of *Accidentally Overweight*

You need to read this whole book. Do not just go to the solutions section of each chapter as you won't understand *why* specific changes are being recommended. You also need to read through each chapter because there are solutions offered the whole way through the text and you may miss these if you don't read everything. There is a reason for the order of the chapters.

Information is expanded upon as the book continues and we move from the physical bases of body fat accumulation through to the emotional and along the way you'll see how they are all linked. Nothing stands alone in our chemistry. Also, to truly get the immense benefits from the emotions chapter, you need to know the stories that set this chapter up and which are presented throughout the book. So please read it from cover to cover and soak it up.

Do not go straight to the emotions chapter even if you believe that this is the only part you don't yet understand. *Accidentally Overweight* was written as a sequence, to unfold information and experience when you read it from page one through to the end. Once you have read it all, by all means return to any place you like.

You may notice that throughout the book I often write "we"—it's because I am very used to working as a team with my clients. Even though I am not physically with you as you read this book, I want you to feel like I'm someone who understands. The details of people's lives are very different yet the patterns of responses driving human behavior are often very similar.

There are sections of *Accidentally Overweight* that may seem more geared for a female audience. But the messages in the book are just as relevant to men, even if in certain sections men are simply given the opportunity to better understand the women in their lives. This is particularly true of the chapter on sex hormones.

As I came to better and more deeply evolve my concept of *Accidentally Overweight*, what began as a random scribble on my page grew into a pie chart which I'd ask clients to complete so we could establish the areas in which they needed support.

Although today I use the image of a puzzle to depict the concept of *Accidentally Overweight*, this simply serves to illustrate that often numerous pieces have to come together for an individual to reach their weight loss and health goals.

For you to get the most out of this book, I am going to encourage you to begin where I begin with all of my clients—with the pie chart. As you come to the end of each chapter, I'd like you to score yourself for that particular area, not based on a rating of "good" or "bad" but on a scale of one to ten. Ten indicates that this piece of your chart needs absolutely no support or attention—you have that section sorted—while a score of one indicates that you have identified that this particular area needs a significant amount of support and attention. Once you have scored yourself for each chapter, return to the pie chart, mark your scores in each area, and then color in your wheel. The more white space, the more support you need to focus on that area. Most people notice that if their chart were actually a wheel, it wouldn't be able to turn. It would get stuck in one or more areas.

Identifying the areas in which you need support allows you to focus on the information and solutions most relevant to your health. After you have implemented some or all of the strategies suggested in the section/s relevant to you for four-week periods, you can return to your chart and use a different colored marker to identify your new scores. Your goal is not necessarily to get to ten in all areas. Identify the roadblocks to your fat burning and aim to have more colored areas in your chart. Get your scores (your biochemistry) to a point where your weight loss wheel begins to turn again, generating the health outcomes you desire.

> *"If the answers to what you are searching for were in the places you had already been looking, don't you think you would have found them by now?"* Anonymous

It is time to look at food, health, and your body in a brand new way.

Registered Reader

Congratulations on purchasing
Accidentally Overweight!

The science and understanding of the impact that nutrition has on our bodies is constantly changing as colleagues in the research world continue to make breakthroughs.

By purchasing this book you qualify for our Registered Reader program. Our aim with this Registered Reader program is to ensure that we are able to keep you abreast of the latest developments in health and wellbeing, as well as provide you with a touch point to continue to motivate you to achieve the goals you desire for your health and body.

Please become a registered reader
by visiting:
www.accidentallyoverweight.com

Your Accidentally Overweight Puzzle

A Little Background ...

Before beginning, I wanted to reflect on human history so you can begin to truly appreciate just how miraculous our bodies are and also why human health has shifted so significantly in the past thirty or so years.

I'm not talking about human evolution in the sense of biblical "creation" versus Darwinian "evolution." Instead it is a brief exploration of the major milestones in the evolution of the human body and biochemistry.

Human beings have been on Earth for between 150,000 and 200,000 years. We evolved slowly and steadily over time, and, as nomads, we lived off the land that surrounded us as we moved. We were hunters and gatherers and only the seasons, the climate, and the weather conditions influenced our food choices. Humans ate fresh food precisely the way it came from nature. The diet was based primarily on green leaves, and other more concentrated foods were added when the opportunity arose from our hunting and gathering.

Approximately 7,500 to10,000 years ago, humans started to stay in one place for longer periods of time, and very basic agricultural practices were established. This was the first time we grew crops and the first time in human history that we consumed the milk of other animals. This was also the first time that repetition became significant in the human diet as a result of not having to chase our food down and also having a supply of crops in the field. Our patterns of eating, however, were still based on nature's rhythms, and our produce was seasonal and at the mercy of floods and droughts.

While change continued at a very gradual, steady pace, the chemistry developments in our body could keep up. The next most significant change to our lifestyles came during the nineteenth century because of the Industrial Revolution. Processes were mechanized, and people started to move in big numbers from the country to the cities. There was an enormous reliance on agriculture for food production as population numbers continued to grow, and a day's work now required less movement as people came off the land and worked in the newly developed factories.

Propel forward to today. I believe that when

historians review our time on the planet, they will identify the past two decades—which have included the invention of cell phones and the birth of the Internet—as the most rapid period of change in human history. We now eat out of packets, which have numbers (including additives and preservatives) rather than food-based ingredients all over the labels, and live our lives in front of computers. We don't have to climb stairs, as there are elevators, escalators, and moving walkways. We don't even have to go to the store to buy our food, let alone go into the fields and harvest it or chase it with a spear. We can order it online and have someone deliver it. There is no judgment here. Just a tip of the iceberg observation of how quickly and significantly the world in which we live has changed. We are guinea pigs in so many areas. Never before has a group of people been exposed to pesticides for their entire life. Never before have artificial sweeteners, colors, and preservatives been in our food for the entirety of our lifetimes. I am crossing every finger and toe and even my eyes in the hope that they are safe. My instinct tells me they are not.

We have also witnessed a rapid expansion of the human frame and waistline. As hygiene practices improved, along with nutrition generally, we have literally grown to new heights. Unfortunately, our waistlines have grown too, which is both a sign and a consequence of our times.

At a cellular level, we have basically the same human body as our ancestors. Every generation evolves ever so slightly to be better equipped to inhabit its environment. This rate of evolution, however, is nothing compared to the change of pace in our world. Our conscious minds may have developed to keep up with the times, so that we are able to email while we talk on our cell phone at the same time as we recall we must remember to pick up the children from school, but biochemically we are much the same as we were 150,000 years ago. Still the same, too, is our subconscious mind, which is 40,000 times more powerful than our conscious mind. Your subconscious mind makes your heart beat and your hair grow. It knows how to heal a cut without you having to tell it to do so. Don't you think that is amazing? I do not believe that our nervous systems, which enormously affect every cell of our bodies, every hormonal system, every organ, every aspect of fat burning, have been able to keep up with the rate of change that this time in human history demands of us.

Between our laptops and wireless modems, our cell phones and email systems, we are asking our bodies to go places they have never ever been before.

Never have we had a "mail" system that was immediate. Never have we had too little time to prepare our own food. Never have we held phones to our ears 24/7. We are already beginning to learn of the consequences of some of these behaviors. What we are yet to truly realize en masse in the Western world is that the seeming urgency and the pace at which we are living is a disaster for human health, in particular our nervous systems. Not to mention the quality of the "immediate" food that goes along with this immediate lifestyle.

We are so far removed from our origins that you can now eat a tomato in the middle of winter if you choose. As silly and insignificant as that sounds—and of course there are much more destructive food habits than eating a tomato in winter, as tasteless as they may be—it is a clear indication that we have lost touch with the guiding light of nature when it comes to not just our food but also our whole way of living. And in my opinion, Mother Nature knows best. Once, not so long ago, we treated colds with garlic and lemons. Now, we take a pill and race on. I could be on my soapbox for weeks! Essentially, it takes awareness and a commitment to eat with the seasons, even if you do so only some of the time, and it is certainly a challenge to truly rest in this age of immediacy. Yet rest we must.

We now ask our glands and organs, our livers, our gall bladders, our kidneys, our adrenals, our thyroids, our ovaries, our testes, our brains, and our digestive system to cope with whatever we consume in our rush. There are, of course, consequences to this superfast pace of living and this book has been partly borne out of my observations and reflections, as well as the science I have learnt about what this period in our evolution is requiring of us.

We are not wired to cope with constant pressure, perceived or real, nor are we equipped long-term to eat poor quality food and lead sedentary lifestyles, strapped to our computers, cell phones plugged into our ear sockets. As I said, this is the tip of a partially inglorious but incredibly fascinating iceberg and the Western world needs to ask, "Where to from here?" Let me remind you of what you already know.

Introduction

ccidentally Overweight is about what has to happen for a human to be able to access body fat and burn it. Essentially it is about weight loss and all the things that need to come together in our bodies to make it possible. The ultimate intention behind this book, however, is to free people from their battle with their bodies, a battle that may interfere with them sharing their full gifts with the world. Sound altruistic? Let me explain.

Whether conscious or subconscious, many people are frustrated by how they feel about their body, or its appearance, and this frustration can take up their headspace and influences their moods. This in turn can affect their self-esteem and the way they relate to the people around them. There are days when they feel fine, even quite good and positive, but the next day or even later on the same day, they feel revolting again, often for no obvious reason. They might feel heavy or swollen or sluggish or puffy or bloated or just plain yuck. When we feel that way, do you think we are likely to treat people—including ourselves and the people we love the most in the world—kindly or impatiently? Typically, it is the latter and because those on the receiving end of your frustrations don't usually deserve the behavior you are dishing out, or understand the reasons behind it, they can easily interpret it with meanings about how you feel about them such as "she doesn't love me." Such unintended messages and just being on the receiving end of your impatience or sadness can then go on to influence how they interact with others and feel about themselves. You can see how this vicious cycle can be perpetuated.

Furthermore, when we feel this way about ourselves, do you think we are likely to make excellent or poor food choices? Once again, the latter is the likely scenario, which of course only serves to compound our lousy view of ourselves. Yet, such a perspective is usually far from the front of our minds when we make such choices and so we just feel sadder and sadder about ourselves, including our appearance. We may feel like we will never be any different.

The other way I see challenges and frustrations with the body enormously affect a person's world is by the deep sadness that can develop, especially if they have from time to time made massive efforts to eat well and exercise regularly with little or no reward. Such lack of success can drive their gaze inward and take up so much time and focus, again consciously or subconsciously, that they are unable to see that their body is, among many things, a tool through which they can learn. And the lessons on offer are those that can assist the individual as well the world around them. I've come to see that mostly it is never about the body, just as it is never about the food. These are just the vehicles doing their best to wake you up. It is about a bigger picture. And once you've caught even a glimpse of that, let alone truly understood and integrated the insights, your relationship with your body, with food, with your health, and with the people around you will never be the same again.

Imagine waking up and your first thoughts *not* being about what you will or won't eat that day, or how much exercise you will or won't manage to do. Imagine not setting out to eat only this and this and this today but by 4:00 pm or thereabouts inhaling whatever you can get your hands on… and then berating yourself about how useless you are and that you have no willpower. Imagine not doing that ever again!

By exploring the physical mechanisms of your biochemistry and the emotional driving forces in your life, you will understand what has governed the growing and shrinking of your body up until now. And through that understanding and the practical solutions I can offer you, you will have your very own recipe to solve so much more than just your weight loss puzzle. Food will no longer rule you, and your weight will simply fall into place. You will no longer measure or judge yourself by that magic number on the scales. In fact, there is every chance that you will stop weighing yourself altogether because you will naturally feel and look your very best, and you will know in your heart that you don't need a scale to validate anything about your beautiful self.

Digestion
The Basis of Your Health

I t never ceases to amaze me how magnificent and how clever our bodies really are, and it astounds me how many processes go on inside the body without us having to give them any thought. Digestion is one of those processes. The nourishment we are provided as result of good digestion is an extraordinary gift without which we would not survive. It is the process through which we get all of the goodness out of our food. Digestion is intricate and complex and yet relatively robust. And it is intimately connected to how you feel and function every single day, from the energy you feel to the fat you burn, from the texture and appearance of your skin to whether you have a bloated tummy or not, right down to your mood. Digestion is responsible for so much that goes on inside us. If it is a body system that gives you grief, if you are bloated most evenings, if you have intermittent diarrhoea and constipation, or if you get reflux, you can reach a point where you feel like it is how life is always going to be. It must just be how you are. Perhaps you believe it's "in your family." Well, bowel challenges do not have to be your reality.

Digestion is the perfect place to start when solving your weight loss puzzle. It is important that these initial building blocks to outstanding health are in place. It can be a challenge to balance hormones for example, if your digestion is the bane of your life. The gut is essentially like a second brain in your body. Did you know that 80 percent of the body's total serotonin is in the gut? And with serotonin being our primary happy, calm, content hormone, gut dysfunction can enormously affect our mood.

Some of the information in this section may make you giggle...it can be a challenge to find the right words to describe our stools! And some of the advice may at first seem obvious and too simple to make much of a difference. But reflect on your own eating habits and digestive system functions as you read on, and be ready to be Accidentally Overweight no more.

Digestion is the process of breaking down food so that we can absorb and utilise it for energy and to sustain our lives. Food is simply broken down into smaller components. For example, proteins are broken down into amino acids, and it is through this breakdown of food and our absorption of these smaller substances that we are nourished. As I have inferred, it is a process that never ceases to amaze me.

The digestive system is made up of a digestive tract, a big long tube (imagine it looking like a hose) and numerous ancillary organs, including the liver, gall bladder, and pancreas. The illustration on the next page gives you an idea. The big long tube begins at your mouth, moves down the oesophagus, through a valve, and into your stomach. The food then moves through a valve at the bottom side of the stomach into the small intestine, through the small intestine and ileo-caecal valve into the large intestine, and then any waste is excreted out the other end. When this process works well, you look and feel fantastic. When it is in any way impaired, the opposite can be true, and correcting it can change your life.

The Human Digestive System: *The oesophagus enters the stomach (a cut away section is shown above). The tube continues into the small intestine (smooth tube above) and then into the large intestine (the indented tube section above) and the waste is excreted. The liver (L), gallbladder (G) and pancreas (P) are also highlighted above.*

CHEW YOUR FOOD

Food enters the mouth and moves down the oesophagus into the stomach. But what do we do to our food before it reaches the stomach? We chew it or, in some cases, we inhale it! There are no more teeth beyond the mouth. You can't chew it anymore once the food has left your mouth. Yet, so many people eat as though their oesophagus is lined with teeth. Many of us are in such a hurry with our meals or we are so excited by the flavour of our food that we might chew each mouthful four times if we're lucky. It's a case of chew chew chew chew mmmmm yum, next forkful in, chew chew, oh gosh my mouth is so full, better swallow some food...so we swallow some partially chewed food and some not at all chewed food and we do this day in, day out, year after year. And somehow we expect our stomach just to cope.

The stomach gets to a point where it doesn't like the rules by which you are playing anymore, so it takes its bat and goes home. So, slow down! Chew your food! If you are a food inhaler, try this: put food into your mouth, chew it really well, and then swallow it before you put the next mouthful in. I know that sounds simple, but try it. For food inhalers, it can take an enormous amount of concentration to change their eating behaviours. Put your fork or spoon down between each mouthful if that will help. Engage in conversation if you are eating with others. Or, think of your own technique to slow yourself down if you hoover your food. You need to pay attention when you eat and to how you eat.

Now, back to the stomach, the first place food lands after you have swallowed it. Make a fist and look at it. Yes, clench your fist and observe its size. That is how big your stomach is without any food in it. Tiny, isn't it? So, think about what happens when you pile your plate high in the evening and inhale that big mountain of food. Your stomach has to stretch to accommodate it. And food has to sit in the stomach for a minimum of thirty minutes to allow the stomach acid and other digestive juices to really begin to break the food down.

Once your stomach gets used to being stretched, it expects it every day, and this stretching is the reason why, if you decide to eat less or go on a "diet," you tend to feel hungry after your meals for around four days, as it can take a few days for the nerve endings around your stomach pouch to shrink back. The nerves are fired off when they reach a certain stretching point and send a message to the brain to let you know you have eaten.

This is one of the numerous mechanisms we have that has the potential to tell us to stop eating, that we've had enough. Trouble is, for some, the stomach is so used to being stretched, by the time the nerves fire, we may have over eaten and be berating ourselves. This is the process through which carbo-hydrates let us know we have eaten. With fat and protein however, once we have chewed these foods, messages are already being sent from the mouth to the satiety centre of the brain to let us know we are eating. These signals usually reach the brain within five minutes of chewing, while the stomach stretch method can take more like twenty minutes! As an aside, it is important to include fats and/or protein with each meal, as you are likely to eat less and be satisfied with less total food for that meal than if you simply ate carbohydrates on their own.

A rough guide to the amount of food we need to eat at each meal is approximately two fist sizes. That is concentrated food such as proteins or carbo-hydrates. You can and need to add as many greens (non-starch vegetables and/or salad) to that as you like. Although they have a high nutrient content, they are mostly water. Remember that.

For some of us, the key to body fat management is simply eating less total food by reducing our por-tion sizes. So, eat less. Reduce your portion size by one quarter, especially in the evening if you overeat, and see how you feel!

Obviously, many of us know that we need to reduce our portion size or not eat after dinner, yet no matter how hard we seem to try, we can't seem to eat less or stop eating once we start. This is why the "whys" behind our food/eating behaviours need to be explored and chapter 10 does just that.

STOMACH ACID PH

Food arrives at the stomach after you have chewed and swallowed it. The aroma of food, as well as the chewing action itself, stimulates stomach acid production which is an exceptionally important substance when it comes to great digestion. The role of the stomach acid is to break food down. Imagine your food is a big long string of circles as shown in the first row below. It is the job of the stomach acid to go chop, chop, chop and break the circles apart into smaller bunches, as the second row illustrates.

OOOOOOOOOOOOOOOOOOOOOOOO
⇓ (stomach acid)
OOO   OO OOO   OOO   OO   OOOO   OO

Digestion: *The action of stomach acid on whole foods breaks them down into their smaller components.*

Your body is governed by pH ranges. pH is a measure of acidity or alkalinity. In scientific terms, pH refers to the concentration of hydrogen ions present, but you don't need to worry about that to understand this very important process. The pH range is based on a scale from one to fourteen, with one being the acid end of the spectrum and fourteen being the alkaline end, while seven is neutral. Every fluid, every tissue, every cell of your body has a pH at which it performs optimally. The optimal pH of stomach acid is 1.9, which is so acidic it would burn you if it touched your skin. But it doesn't burn you while it is nicely housed inside your stomach, as the cells that line the stomach itself not only produce stomach acid but are also designed to withstand the super acidic conditions.

For many of us, though, the pH of our stomach acid is not acidic enough, and it may have a pH far greater than 1.9, which is not ideal for digestion. To be precise, animal proteins are optimally digested at a pH of 1.9 while starch is optimally digested at a pH of 2.1 which may not seem like much number-wise, but, inside your body, it can mean the difference between a flat abdomen and a bloated abdomen after a meal. A professor in the United States has been researching the pH of stomach acid in various groups of people who have been diagnosed with specific conditions such as children with autism spectrum disorder (ASD). Many children with ASD have been found to have a stomach acid pH of around four, far too high to be effectively digesting protein or starch.

Adults with reflux or indigestion tend to assume that the burning sensation they experience with heartburn means they are producing too much acid when the reality is usually the opposite. They are usually not making enough stomach acid and/or the pH of it is too high. To understand this, remember the food as a string of circles analogy and that stomach acid plays a vital role in breaking the circles apart. A pH that is much higher than 1.9 cannot effectively break the circles apart and larger segments of, for example, seven circles in length may be the result. The body knows that if something that is seven circles in length continues along the digestive tract, it is not going to be able to further digest these partially broken down circles. Rather than allowing that food to proceed down into the small intestine for the next part of its journey, the body regurgitates the food in an attempt to get rid of it. We then experience the acid burn and assume it is too acidic when, in fact, it is not acidic enough to break the food down properly and allow it to pass into the small intestine. It "burns" you, because anything with an acid pH that is too acidic for the tissue to which is exposed will create a burning sensation. When the acid is contained inside the stomach pouch, all is well, however, when it escapes out of this area, the lining of the oesophagus and the first part of the small intestine are not designed to cope with such acidic contents. Many people with reflux respond very well to the stimulation of stomach acid (and/or the omittance of problem foods for them) and experience much fewer symptoms as a result.

As mentioned, stomach acid is stimulated by chewing, the aroma of food, as well as by the consumption of lemon juice and apple cider vinegar (ACV). The chewing action sends a message to the brain to send a message to the stomach to let it know that food is on its way. When we inhale our food, this doesn't happen. Historically, we regularly took much longer to prepare our meals and the slow cooking processes generated an aroma of the upcoming meal, again signalling to the stomach that food was on its way. Lemon juice and ACV physically stimulate the production of stomach acid. If you haven't consumed either of these before, it is best to initially dilute them and ideally consume them five to twenty minutes before breakfast (or all of your main meals if that appeals). For example, you might begin with half a teaspoon of ACV in as much water as you like. Over the coming days and weeks, gradually work up to having one tablespoon of ACV while you gradually decrease the amount of water. If you would prefer lemon juice, start with the juice of half a lemon diluted to your tastes with warm water and gradually work up to having the juice of a whole lemon in less warm water. As an aside, it can be a good idea to brush your teeth after your meals when you use lemon to prevent any potential problems with tooth enamel in the future. Use these tips to wake your stomach acid up before you eat!

THE POTENTIAL EFFECT OF DRINKING WATER WITH MEALS

We need the pH of our stomach acid to sit around two. Water has a pH of seven (neutral pH) or above, depending on the mineral content (the higher the mineral content, the higher/more alkaline the pH). When you add a liquid with a pH of seven or more to one with a pH of two, what do you potentially do to the stomach acid? You dilute it. And we need all of the digestive fire we can muster to get the maximum nourishment out of our food and the best out of us. In my ideal world, we wouldn't drink water thirty minutes either side of eating.

When I'm giving a seminar on this topic, at this point in the presentation, a member of the audience invariably shouts out, "what about wine?" Wine has a more acidic pH than water, so although it puts a load on the liver, from a digestion perspective, it takes less of a toll than water. Usually, at that point in the seminar, I am everybody's new best friend!

You do not need to be concerned about the water

content of food, nor do you need to focus on omitting all beverages at every meal time. Simply aim to drink water between meals, not with meals! It can be a challenging habit to break. Set yourself a goal of not drinking with meals for one week...and then preferably keep the new habit going. Or, add a squeeze of fresh lemon juice if you insist on water with your meal for your own reasons. Just cut it out for a week, (one little week out of your very long life) and see if you feel any different.

PH GRADIENT OF THE DIGESTIVE SYSTEM

Once food has been somewhat broken down in the stomach, it moves through the pyloric sphincter, a one-way valve leading into the duodenum, which is the beginning of the small intestine. Physically, in your body, this valve is located in the middle (or just slightly on the left) of the chest, just below where a lady's bra sits and just below a man's pectoral muscles.

While food is in the stomach, messages are being sent to the pancreas to secrete sodium bicarbonate (as well as digestive enzymes), which has a highly alkaline pH. The bicarbonate is designed to protect the lining of the first part of the small intestine as well as to allow digestion to continue. What is known as a "pH gradient" is established all the way along the digestive tract, and each region of the big long tube has an ideal pH. When the pH gradient is not established in the stomach, that is, when the pH is higher than ideal, digestion problems are likely further along the tract. These may be symptoms of the small or large intestine, such as bloating, pain, or excessive wind. It also means that the absorption of nutrients may be compromised. Insufficient pancreatic bicarbonate production may also cause digestive symptoms such as a burning sensation underneath the stomach in the valve area described above. Pain in this area can also indicate that the gall bladder needs some support or investigation. It is best to consult with your health professional about this if you feel discomfort in this area.

The best way to let the pancreas know that it needs to jump to action and produce bicarbonate and digestive enzymes is to have good stomach acid production at optimal pH. The digestive system runs off a cascade of signals from one organ or area to the next, via the brain. Use the suggested strategies, especially chewing food well, to stimulate the pancreas to fulfil its role.

There are occasions when I have suggested clients use supplements of pancreatic enzymes, and this is appropriate if there is a genuine lack rather than simply poor stomach acid conditions. I usually suggest the aforementioned strategies before trialling supplements however, when symptoms are severe and once other causes have been ruled out, a gastroenterologist may measure pancreatic enzyme levels.

ABSORPTION

As food moves through the small bowel, digestive enzymes are secreted from the pancreas and the brush border (lining) of the small intestine. The role of these enzymes is to continue what the stomach acid began which is to continue to break down the food we have eaten into its smallest, most basic components. It is in the small intestine where you absorb all of the goodness (vitamins and minerals) out of your food. Think about that. All of the goodness, all of the nutrients that keep you alive, are drawn out of your food and into your blood so that your body can use those nutrients to do all of the life sustaining jobs they do. Alcohol and vitamin B12 are virtually the only substances you absorb directly out of your stomach (rather than your small intestine) into your blood. Alcohol tends to be in your blood within five minutes of consuming it, which is why humans may get tipsy if they drink it on an empty stomach.

So the small intestine is where the nutrients in your food move from the tube that is your digestive tract into the blood, which is obviously a different set of tubes. This is how we are nourished, and it is how you stay alive!

Just because you eat something, though, doesn't mean you get all of the goodness out of it. Just because a food contains, for example, ten milligrams of zinc, doesn't mean you will get (absorb) the whole ten milligrams when you eat it. The absorption of nutrients is dependent on a whole host of factors, some of which have been discussed above. If you inhale your food, drink water with your meals, or have poor stomach acid production, for example, you may absorb very little of the goodness in your food. And if you think that through, nutrients are essential for life and simply as a result of the way you are eating, let alone the foods you might be choosing, you may be robbing yourself of some of the goodness your food provides. Give yourself the best opportunity to absorb as much goodness out of your food as possible through applying the tips above! It may add energy to your years and years to your life.

IS THAT NIGGLING PAIN IN YOUR SIDE APPENDICITIS?

So many of my clients describe to me an on again off again pain that hits them quite low down on the right hand side of their abdomen. If you place your little finger on your right hip bone and use your thumb to find your navel, this pain tends to be located about half way in between on that diagonal line. This is the ileo-caecal valve, where the small intestine meets the large intestine. Many people have mistaken illeo-caecal valve pain for appendicitis, as the appendix is located not far from this area. Always see a medical professional to diagnose your pain.

For many, pain begins in this area after a tummy bug (infection) or so often after travelling, usually overseas or camping, and having diarrhoea, or after a bout of food poisoning. Even though the obvious symptoms of the causative infection have long since gone, it is as if the nasty little critters that caused the original upset tummy have taken up residence in the valve. Or perhaps they have changed its function. To remedy this pain, there are numerous options to try. One is to release the reflex connected to this valve by rubbing the area with your finger tips twenty times in an anticlockwise circular motion with reasonable pressure, not so it hurts you but also not with fairy fingers. Another option is to use anti-parasitic herbs such as Chinese Wormwood and Black Walnut for four to eight weeks every day, before each main meal. The other potential remedy is one of my favourite substances on Earth, Lugol's iodine. The liquid of potassium iodide is not only a source of iodine, necessary for so many body functions, but it acts as a potent anti-parasitic agent that seems to help clear the last of the nasty critters from this important valve. It is possible to overdose on iodine so it is best to check your dosage with a health professional to make sure the dose is right for you.

GUT BACTERIA

Now that the food has progressed through to the large intestine, can you guess what lives in here? Bacteria. On average, an adult will have three to four kilograms of bacteria living in their colon. So, just as an aside, every time you weigh yourself remember that three to four of the kilos you see in that number on the scales is made up of gut bacteria that are essential for life. See how crazy it is that we weigh ourselves. All you do when you weigh yourself is weigh your self-esteem. More on that in later chapters.

Some of the bacteria in your large bowel (colon) are good guys and some are bad guys. You want more good guys than bad guys. The role of the gut bacteria is to ferment whatever you give them. To come back to the circle concept of food illustrated previously, gut bugs love it when you give them something that is one or even two circles in size.

They know what to do with that. But if a previous digestive process has not been completed sufficiently, the gut bacteria in our colon may be presented with fragments of food that are five or even seven circles in size, and all they know to do with any food they are offered is to ferment it.

What word springs to mind when you think of fermentation? I love asking this question at my seminars, as the answers usually amuse me as well as the audience. People will often say "beer," "wine," "sauerkraut"! But usually I get the answer I'm after, which is gas. Fermentation involves bacterial action on a food source and the subsequent production of gas. Some gases are essential to the health of the cells that line our gut while others seem to irritate the gut and give us a bloated, uncomfortable stomach as the day progresses, whether we have eaten in a "healthy" way or not.

The trouble with a bloated stomach for many women (in particular) is that it messes with their brain. When they look down and see a swollen tummy, something inside immediately communicates to every cell of their body that they are fat, whether they consciously think this thought or not. Many of my clients go up a size around the waist as the day progresses even though they feel they have eaten with their health in mind. This can add a layer of stress to a person's life that they just don't need or understand. It is especially stressful because they can't fathom why it is happening. Sometimes it is the foods you are choosing. Sometimes it is the bugs that are living in your colon. Sometimes it is because of poor digestion further up the process such as insufficient stomach acid. In Traditional Chinese Medicine (TCM), this is considered a spleen and/or liver picture and a TCM practitioner is likely to use acupuncture and/or herbs to support the spleen and liver.

STRESS

Poor digestion can also be due to stress or, more precisely, adrenalin. Adrenaline diverts the blood supply away from your digestive processes and concentrates the blood in your periphery, your arms and legs. The reason for this is that not having blood focussed on digestion is more likely to get you out of the perceived danger you are in, and it keeps you focussed on escaping the danger. If blood were still concentrated on the digestive system, there is a risk you would be distracted by food and, again, if you really were in danger, which is what adrenaline communicates to your body, your life may be over if you suddenly spotted a piece of fruit hanging in a tree nearby rather than remaining focussed on getting out of danger. Stress, stress hormones, and the processes they drive in your body, including those related to body fat, weight loss, and digestion, are explored in great detail later in this book.

BOWEL EVACUATION

In dealing with clients one-on-one, I have had to work out ways to extract information from people using "appropriate" language and also with words that accurately investigate what is going on for that person. Many years ago, one of the questions I originally found difficult to phrase was around how empty someone felt after they had used their bowels. I tried to dream up ways to word this question so that it wouldn't make clients feel uncomfortable (not that many of them are concerned!) but also so that I could gain more insight into how their bowel was functioning. As with most things, a client turned out to be my teacher; he had the answer. While asking him about his bowel habits, he said, "You know what? My greatest discomfort comes from incomplete evacuation." There they were. The words I needed. So, early on in my consultation work with people, I started asking about feelings of incomplete evacuation. For some, it's not an issue at all. They have no idea what I'm talking about when I mention it. For others, they are so excited that someone has finally given them the words to describe such frustrating discomfort. They wouldn't answer yes if I asked them if they were constipated, as they may use their bowels every day. It is just that when they do go to the toilet, they feel like there is more to come but it doesn't eventuate and evacuate.

This feeling can be the result of numerous scenarios. It may be insufficient digestive processes as outlined previously. It may be inadequate production of digestive enzymes due to poor signalling or a damaged or inflamed brush border. It may be a food allergy or intolerance. It may be poor fibre intake or dehydration. It can be stress hormones causing the muscles surrounding the bowel to contract and hold onto waste. It may be a magnesium deficiency not allowing the walls of the bowel to relax and allow the thorough passage of waste. The thyroid gland may not be working optimally. TCM teaches us it is insufficient spleen and/or liver energy. The list of scenarios is almost endless.

One option to improve this challenge is to have a health professional help you get to the bottom of it and remedy the situation. You might increase the green vegetables and decrease the processed foods in your diet for a week and see if that makes a difference, especially given that green vegetables are good sources of magnesium, water and fibre, amongst other things. You may be suspicious of a food or a group of foods that are causing this feeling for you but because you love this food you are reticent to remove it. I cannot encourage you enough to remove your suspicious food from your diet for a trial period of two weeks (four is even better). Two little weeks out of your very long life, an expression I use regularly with clients to highlight the relatively short time period necessary to potentially offer enormous insight into their health challenges. You may get an answer to your challenge over the trial period and, if not, you can relax and thoroughly enjoy this food that you love rather than silently wondering if it is the basis of your incomplete evacuation. But I can hear you already asking..."what if it works...what does that mean...will I never eat that food again?" My answer is always that it is your choice.

I've witnessed people be so resistant to dietary change and after a time they feel so different, so much better that they have no desire to ever go back to the way they used to eat. I meet others who miss a food terribly. If it is the latter scenario, I suggest to that person after the trial, that now they know. It is no longer a mystery to them why they feel this way. Then they are in control. Unless the problem is a true allergy, I find that when people are strong, meaning when they are very robust from a digestion perspective, their gut will tolerate this food better than if they are stressed. Either way, once you know, you are in control, and it is your choice. You know that if you have an important event coming up, you might like to avoid the culprit food for a time so you feel and look your best for your occasion. Again, unless the food is a true allergy for you, your tolerance of it may change and improve over time, especially with a focus on gut healing and stress management. Don't think that because it hurts you today it always will. Your body changes and renews itself constantly. Just know there is a reason for your symptom. It is simply a matter of finding your answer.

One of the reasons I'm so concerned with bowel evacuation is that if this process is inefficient, waste can remain inside the bowel for too long. While it is there, it is fermenting. This can give the liver additional and unnecessary toxin to process as well as "suffocating" the cells that line the colon. The waste can also dry out and harden, sticking itself to the lining of the bowel wall, narrowing the tube through which the new waste can flow. If you have ever seen soil in the middle of a drought, cracked, dried out, and unable to absorb a brief shower of rain, that is the way hardened faeces can behave in your colon.

If this scenario occurs, waste can only move through the middle of this newly formed, faeces lined tube, and the efficiency of waste elimination is decreased. The old, hard, compacted faecal matter remains. When the cells that line the bowel are coated with hard faeces, they are unable to "breathe," and a process that was once described in medical textbooks as "autointoxication" ensues. To remedy this, chamomile is one of the best things you can take. Either drink lots of tea, or take capsules with each meal. Once the waste has dried out, it is difficult to rehydrate it so it can move through and be excreted. Chamomile softens the waste and helps the bowel wall relax.

Another remedy is one that many people have very strong opinions about, colon hydrotherapy or colonics as they are known. This process involves a tube being inserted into a person's rectum through which warm or cool water gently flows. This allows the hardened faecal matter to soften, like heavy, consistent rain on dried out soil, allowing the large bowel to empty fully, often getting rid of built up waste that may have been there for a very long time. I have had clients tell me that the waste they excreted during their first colonic was black, inferring that it may have been there for many years, interfering with healthy bowel function. I had a lady once tell me she saw popcorn in the "viewing" pipe during her colonic and she knows that the last time she ate popcorn was at the movies with her now ex-boyfriend whom she hadn't been with for over six months!

Colonics polarise people. The idea either appeals to you or it doesn't. There is no middle ground with people's love or dislike of colon hydrotherapy. I will encourage you, though, to not lose sight of what trends have done to medicine. Up until the early 1900s, colonics were part of general medicine, and doctors understood the importance of good bowel evacuation. When you examine the history of medicine and observe the split between what we now know to be Western medicine and Complementary medicine, it is clear why this happened, however this book does not seek to explore this segregation in detail. I will simply say that colonics were once accepted as a very "normal" treatment method for a host of health conditions, not just bowel issues. With a well-functioning bowel, an enormous load is not only taken off the digestive system but also the liver, the organ primarily responsible for cleaning our body. Help prevent bowel cancer by ensuring efficient bowel evacuation using methods that suit you! Always seek advice from a health professional before undertaking colon hydrotherapy if it appeals to you.

An additional concept within digestive health that is not only fascinating but has wide-ranging effects on how we feel and function, including gut transit time (how quickly food moves through the digestive system), mood, concentration, and, potentially, food addictions, is a concept known as the opioid excess theory.

The cells that line a healthy small intestine look like a row of neatly stacked bricks with finger-like projections (called villi), side-by-side as demonstrated in the picture below.

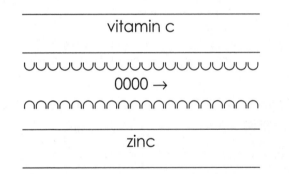

A Healthy Gut: *Food (circles) travelling through a healthy mature intestine move straight ahead. Only nutrients (e.g. Vitamin C and zinc) enter the blood vessels that closely follow the intestines.*

In a healthy gut, only the tiny nutrients (vitamins and minerals) diffuse (move) through the gut wall into the blood, and this is the precious process through which we are nourished and stay alive. However, the cells that line the gut can come apart, as if the bricks are stacked with gaps, illustrated below. This is, in fact, how we are born.

```
_____
              _____
∪ ∪  ∪ ∪∪  ∪ ∪∪∪  ∪∪ ∪∪  ∪∪∪ ∪  ∪
         0000000 → or ↓
∩ ∩∩∩  ∩∩  ∩ ∩∩   ∩∩ ∩↓ ∩∩∩  ∩∩
_____↓_____
         0000000
_____
```

A "Leaky" Gut: Food (circles) travel through an immature gut or a "leaky" intestine. Microscopic, poorly digested fragments of food can escape out of the gut and enter the blood.

When we are born, the cells that line our digestive system are a distance apart which is why we can't feed all foods to newborns; foods must be gradually introduced to a child over time to prevent allergic reactions as the gut matures. The gut is immature when we are born, and it slowly matures from birth until reaching full maturity somewhere between the ages of two and five, depending on the individual child and their health and life experiences in the early years. The cells that line the gut can, however, also come apart during adulthood as a result of a gastrointestinal infection or stress.

The chronic production of stress hormones can compromise the integrity of the gut cells and signal to them that they need to move further apart so that more nutrition can get through to the blood, as nutrient requirements increase during times of stress. Everything about us is geared for survival.

When food travels through a gut with good cell lining integrity, it can only go straight ahead. However, if it travels through a gut in which the cells have come apart, it may go straight ahead or it may move out of the gut and into the blood. Fragments of food are not intended to enter the blood. Nutrients are, the vitamins and minerals from food. If fragments of food enter the bloodstream, the immune system, which is what protects you from infection, thinks that the food fragment is a germ and it mounts an immune response against it. This is one way adults develop food sensitivities. Poor gut integrity is also described as "leaky gut." Once you were able to eat anything without a problem, and now certain foods seem to cause you grief. This process can be healed by minimising the irritation to the gut lining which can mean avoiding some foods or ingredients for a period of time while also working on the gut integrity. Often people are able to tolerate the foods that cause them grief once we have worked out why they have the "leaky gut" symptoms in the first place. Did the problem begin as a result of stress or an infection? The power to heal the symptoms is always in the why.

The blood supply into which the food fragments flow is the same blood supply that goes to your brain. Humans have what is known as the blood-brain barrier (BBB), a semi-permeable layer separating the peripheral blood supply from that of the brain. The BBB was always considered to be a highly selective membrane that only allowed substances into the brain that would be of benefit. Research has now shown us that this is not the case. In cases where gut permeability is increased, the BBB is often suspected of having the same increased permeability. Further reading about this topic is noted in the References section at the end of the book.

If we could literally see the food fragments, their structure is very similar to that of the opioids. Opioids are substances that help humans feel good. They also modulate pain. We have our own natural feel good hormones that have an opioid-based structure called endorphins. In our brain and in our gut, we have what are called opioid receptors. Just because your body makes a substance (chemical messenger/hormone) doesn't mean you necessarily get the effects of that substance. The substance must bind to a receptor, just like a lock and a key fitting together, for you to get the effect generated by that hormone. In this case, when we make endorphins and they bind to the opioid receptors, we feel pleasure. Heroine and morphine are opioids and they too bind to the opioid receptors in the brain. Anything that gives a human pleasure has the potential to be addictive. Hence, a human's capacity to be addicted to the aforementioned drugs. You can also see from this example how someone might become addicted to exercise. Activity certainly generates endorphins when we partake. So whatever spins your tyres, like a sunset, a spin class, a football game, or a child's laughter, what has happened in that moment is that you have made endorphins and they have bound to opioid receptors, and you have felt pleasure.

How does this relate to food? Some of the fragments of food that can escape out of a leaky gut into the bloodstream can also have an opioid structure. Their names include beta-casomorphine and gluteomorphine. They are partially digested fragments of casein, the major protein in cow's milk products, and gluten, the major protein in wheat, rye, barley, oats and triticale. Just like endorphins, these opioids from food also have the capacity to bind to the opioid receptors in the brain and very subtly make us feel good. The effect is not usually noticed as an enormous boost in mood, but the person will often feel like they can't live without this food, and they will have to eat it in some form daily or even at every meal.

I have seen this to be the case with countless clients. If a patient has a set of symptoms that warrants them omitting a food from their diet for a trial period to see if it will make a difference, some people have no problem. There is no resistance. Others will beg me not to take them off a food, yet they are seeing me because they want results, and all I am asking is four measly weeks of omitting a particular food that may just give them the answer to some of their health concerns! I am not judging someone who responds in this way. I am simply pointing out to you that the power food can have over an individual is just like an addiction. Their connection to it, their need for it, is often highly emotional and also potentially physical through this opioid mechanism.

Food was never intended to fill these roles for humans. Yet, on a physical level, it is possible that the opioid effect some foods have the potential to create when a leaky gut is occurring, is one of the factors behind food addictions and, hence, for some, overeating or eating and not feeling like you can stop. This is an area that deserves much more research, time, and money as the opioid excess theory may be involved in numerous health conditions as well as obesity. Much research has already been done in relation to children with autism and adults with schizophrenia where these "exorphins" (opioids from an exogenous (consumed from outside as opposed to having been made by the body) source) have been found to play a role in the expression of symptoms of these conditions. Food not only has the capacity to affect our body shape and size but also our mood, and our digestion of some foods may be incomplete, leading to the generation of an opioid effect and addiction to particular foods. If you suspect this process is going on for you, omit all sources of that dietary component (gluten and/or casein) for a trial period of four weeks. The first four to seven days will be the most difficult, but persevere. The results may be enormously worth it. If you do omit significant dietary components from your diet for extended periods, it can be useful to consult a health professional to make sure you do not miss out on any nutrients essential for your health.

TCM PERSPECTIVE ON DIGESTION

The spleen rules digestion in TCM. TCM considers that each organ has its own vital energy as well as there being a whole body energy. If spleen energy is down, you will feel your usual hunger for meals, but as soon as you eat even a small amount, you will feel full and possibly bloated. Your short term memory is likely to not be what it once was, and you may possibly feel like you eat like a bird yet your weight continues to escalate. You can eat and exercise with a real commitment, but if spleen energy is low, from a TCM perspective, you may not budge a kilo.

Stimulating spleen energy can make a real difference. Acupuncture will do this as will bitter herbs. Spleen energy will go low in the first place from what is simply described as over-thinking. The busy mind, relentlessly thinking of the next thing you need to do, takes energy away from the vital process of digestion every day, according to TCM principles. The spleen may also lose some of its strength if liver or kidney (adrenals sit on top of the kidneys) energy is over-bearing or low. Working with a wonderful TCM practitioner can also assist you heal your gut.

CONCLUSION OF DIGESTION AND A SUMMARY OF THE SOLUTIONS

Digestion is central and essential to every process in our body which is why, although Digestion is not a weight loss puzzle piece on its own, I wanted you to read this section first, as it is the base from which we build. So, whether your focus is weight loss, optimising your health and wellbeing, and/or improving a challenging or diseased gut, understanding your digestive system is a crucial step on our way to exploring even more fascinating aspects of your health and solving your weight loss puzzle.

Remember to:

- Slow down! Chew your food.

- Include fats and/or protein with each meal as you are likely to eat less and be satisfied with less total food for that meal, than if you simply eat carbohydrates on their own.

- Eat less. Reduce your portion size by one quarter, especially in the evening if you overeat and see how you feel.

- Wake your stomach acid up before you eat by using lemon juice in warm water or apple cider vinegar before meals, breakfast in particular.

- Drink water between meals, not with meals.

- Use the strategies throughout Accidentally Overweight to ensure efficient bowel evacuation.

- Omit a food you feel you cannot live without for a trial period of four weeks. The first four to seven days will be the most difficult but persevere. The results may be enormously worth it.

- Working with a wonderful TCM practitioner can also assist you heal your gut.

- Try Aloe Vera juice to start your day if you have a particularly irritated gut.

- Eat in a calm state.

- Look at the food while you eat it. Do not read or watch TV while you eat.

Calories
Puzzle Piece Number 1

M ost of us have been taught that body shape and size is simply a matter of calories in versus calories burned. For many of us, in the early part of our life this appears to be absolutely true. Yet for some, eating less or exercising more may not seem to make the difference it once did. For some, it makes no difference at all and no matter whether they put in maximum effort or zero effort with food or exercise, their bodies remain overweight or in a state of constant expansion. People can be very quick to blame age, but if age were truly a factor then surely every eighty-year-old would be overweight. Instead, what I have witnessed every day of my working life is the impact numerous body systems have on metabolism—either as a result of lifestyle choices, life experiences, or pressure, whether real or perceived. Most frequently, all of these factors play a role. Only without emotion would our body shape and size be completely reliant on the calorie equation.

YOU KNOW YOU NEED TO EAT LESS...

You cannot eat like a piglet and expect everything to fall into place. That's just common sense. You would have to have had your head buried in the sand for the past thirty years not to know we need to eat more fresh fruits and vegetables and less processed food, and we all know it's not healthy to sit on our bottom all day. Yet I have met thousands of people who exercise frequently, often intensely—many, even every day of the week—and still their body fat levels don't change or, heaven forbid, they slowly increase. It saddens me to hear stories of people who have made a great commitment to eat well and exercise regularly, yet their bodies didn't change. If you set out on your healthy regime to drop a clothes size and this doesn't happen, it can be disheartening. When that happens people often throw all of their good intentions out the window. We forget about the other important benefits of exercise, such as improved bone density, lymphatic stimulation, clarity of thought, improved circulation and, potentially, a deeper connection with nature, to name but a few. Just because we haven't dropped a clothes size or been noticeably rewarded for our efforts, we can easily wonder what the point is and give up.

Most humans are very black and white when it comes to food and exercise. Either we commit to regular exercise and eating well—choosing healthy meals and not much, if any, takeout—or we are sitting on the couch, not caring about what we put into our mouths, thinking to ourselves as we reach for the fourth chocolate cookie "Oh who cares, I've already blown it." For most people, real life happens somewhere in the grey area in between these two extremes. The problem is that even though we set out with a commitment to eat well and exercise regularly, too often we don't put an end date or progress review date on our plan.

Lots of people make big decisions to eat well and exercise regularly only to find themselves, three weeks later, after a late day at work, buying takeout, polishing off a bottle of wine, falling asleep on the couch, and topping it all off by skipping exercise the morning after. Because they made a decision three weeks ago to eat well and exercise regularly, most people will berate themselves, feel like they have failed, and generally feel blue. Yet if your best friend came into work the next day and described the challenging afternoon she'd had at work the day before, combined with the fact that she worked late, bought takeout, polished off a bottle of wine, fell asleep on the couch, and didn't get up for morning exercise despite the fact that she'd told herself weeks earlier that she was going to eat well and exercise regularly... what would you say? Perhaps something along the lines of, "Oh don't worry, you'll be alright. Today is a new day." Or perhaps something more like "It was just one night, does it really matter?" Yet when we do it, we feel like it's the end of the world. And when you're buried up to your neck with guilt, feeling like it is the end of the world, are you more or less likely to make better food choices that following evening? Exactly. You're far more likely to do it all over again because you feel like you've ruined it. But you haven't ruined anything. If, on the other hand, you see what unfolded the night before as a part of life, or as already in the past, or good for your soul, you are far more likely to grin and then take better care of yourself the next night and get back into your exercise the following morning. If you dig yourself into a hole filled with guilt and self-loathing and frustration, it may be days, weeks, months, or even years before you step up and commit to looking after your physical health again.

See the night before for what it was . . . one night. A "grey" night. This is part of real life for most people. And I can tell you right now that the guilt you feel and the harsh self-talk are far worse for you than any takeout or bottle of wine will ever be. It is what you do every day that has an impact on your health, not what you do sometimes. You would never berate a friend the way you berate yourself.

Commit this statement to memory: *Without your health, you have nothing.* For so many, it takes a crisis before you sit back and reflect that you've known for a long time that lifestyle changes needed to be made. You're probably even thinking of whatever it is you need to change as you read this. Whether this change is to eat less sugar or drink less caffeine or alcohol, you know better than anyone. Make these changes now. Not tomorrow, not on Monday, right now. You know better than any health professional the changes you need to make. And as you continue through this book, different issues will begin to come up for you. As you read, things will fly into your head that are relevant to you. For example, you really know you need to eat less sugar, or perhaps you know that coffee doesn't suit you since it makes your heart race and you get the shakes when you drink it. If this is the kind of physical reaction you have, do you really think your body is saying to you, "Gosh, I'm glad you drank that"?

Your body does not have a voice. It can only give you symptoms to let you know whether it is happy or not. So pay attention to the signals your body gives you. Take reflux as an example. If there is a food that gives you reflux, think about what reflux is: you swallow some food and your body is bringing it back up. Do you really think your body is saying, "I'm so glad you just ate that, please eat some more."? No, in fact it's saying just the opposite! Your brain will sometimes try to override your body with comments such as "Oh, but I love it, I can't *not* eat that food," convincing you that your love of a certain food is more important than any discomfort the consumption of that food may cause.

When it comes to food, we think in black and white. Your body isn't saying you're never going to eat this food again. It's simply saying "Not right now, not today, perhaps not even next week—but *not necessarily* never again." Reduce, or take a break from, the foods and drinks you know do not serve you well. Or only eat them when you know you are calm and able to eat slowly or when you are in great company. Keep in mind that it is what you do *every* day that impacts your health, not what you do sometimes, and see if that makes a difference. Support digestive processes in the ways suggested in the section on digestion, and see if that makes a difference. But do not relentlessly continue consuming the food or drinks that drive your body to speak to you with negative consequences. No matter what, make an attempt to truly hear your body.

Food was designed to energize us. Yet many of us seem to have forgotten that. If you feel like you need to fall asleep after a meal, then that meal may not have served you (unless it was high in substances, such as tryptophan, that actually induce sleep). Pay attention to how food makes you feel. Notice if a meal that is denser with protein or a meal that is higher in carbohydrates energizes you or makes you fall asleep. There is no easier time to do this than at breakfast. Does an egg at breakfast energize and sustain you? Or does it nauseate you? Notice these things. Does a grain-based breakfast, porridge, for example, sustain you through to lunchtime, or are you gasping for morning tea only an hour after you eat? Does porridge make you sleepy, or does it make you feel like you could run a marathon? Pay attention. Food is designed to energize you, not exhaust you. A great question to ask yourself before you eat is, "Will this nourish me?" This is something that can be answered from a nutritional perspective, which reflects on the food's vitamin and mineral content, or from a "soul" perspective. Sometimes eating a bag of chips with a glass of wine in the company of your dearest friends is the best thing ever. But, from my perspective, just not every day!

...BUT SOMETIMES YOU CAN'T STOP: EMOTIONAL OVEREATING

Finish this sentence: Food is...

For so many people, the type of word they use to finish this sentence is one relating to pleasure. For example, food is... delicious. Food is... amazing. Food is... yummy. If I ask an athlete that question, they will almost always say food is fuel or food is energy. My own response to that question is food is nourishment. It is nourishment for my body, mind, and soul. A chef I know says food is love. A child I know says food is to make me big and strong. What's the point of this question?

If the answer is a word linked to pleasure, you are far more likely to overconsume. My next question, if you answered with a pleasure word, would be to explore what else in your life currently gives you pleasure. Because if I am going to suggest you change the way you eat and, without realizing it, I suggest you avoid eating all the foods you link to pleasure, we need to help you identify activities or states of being that can replace the pleasure you find in that food, or you won't be able stick to the plans we make. This is one of the main reasons diets don't work. Food is never the problem. It is the reason *behind* your poor food choices or desire for large portions that needs exploring and adjusting. Many of the people who have battled their weight for a long time don't believe they have easy access to other pleasurable thoughts or activities. Food is the easy option. Trouble is, pleasure on the lips is short-lived because deep inside they know what they are eating or the way they are eating is hurting them. They just don't know how to change it.

An athlete for whom food is simply fuel will rarely overeat to the point that it damages their health or performance. Granted, they may miss out on the pleasure that an appreciation of the combination of amazing colors, flavors, and textures on a plate can offer, but someone who views food as fuel rarely eats too much. For me, with the question "will this nourish me?" the one I unconsciously ask before consuming anything (not that I realized this until I started working with people to solve their weight loss challenges), I almost always choose, without thinking, the nutrient-rich, real food option, and I love every mouthful. In other words, the pleasure factor for me when I choose whole foods is enormous. I just don't consciously think it through. My sub-conscious focus is the nourishment. There are times, of course, when I will sit with some corn chips (organic, mind you) in a bowl while I look out across the ocean and, in that moment, the whole scene acts as nourishment for my soul. There is no guilt, no second thought about whether I made a good choice to eat corn chips—and my body size is not affected by a bowl of corn chips on the occasions I choose to eat them. I don't think like that. I pay attention while I eat. I notice and appreciate the crunch of every mouthful I take, and I'm focused on how grateful I feel for the vista in front of me. This concept of being grateful and taking pleasure is important. If all I did was tell you to eat less then, if you are a food is pleasure person, you may feel challenged sustaining this long-term. When you first change your diet and start eating nutrient-rich foods instead of processed, high sugar, trans fat-laden non-foods, you need to be able to connect with or focus on something you are grateful for. It might be the shine in your child's eyes, your dog's playful nature, ears that can hear, eyes that can see, fingers that can touch, a nose that can smell, a roof over your head, or the magnificence of the day you are a part of... focus on these things that light up your heart while you eat, and your brain will start to link your new way of eating to pleasure.

Some people know they eat too much. They know there are too many calories going in for them to be able to manage their body fat, but no matter how many promises of dietary change they make to themselves, they never seem able to follow through. They feel unable to control what they think is their appetite. Without them realizing it, this appetite for food is nearly always an appetite to feel differently, to feel an emotion other than the one wanting to rear its head. Yet at the time all they know is that they feel like eating lots of ice cream!

Say someone is eating too much—perhaps in the form of too many crackers with cheese before dinner, a big dinner itself, or a pint of chocolate chip ice cream after dinner. If I meet with them for a one-on-one consultation and suggest they do this less often or not at all, they would do it for a period of time, partly because they had made an appointment to come and see me and they may have had to wait, they have paid me money for the consultation and so on, so there is a degree of commitment to the dietary changes we design. Because I've seen this pattern countless times, I use the consultation to immediately begin to discover whether the drive for the additional food is physical or emotional or, most likely, both.

On a physical level, chunks of cheese on way too

many crackers may relieve dire hunger, yet if that person had eaten afternoon tea they would almost certainly be able to wait until dinner without inhaling a predinner dinner of cheese and crackers. But with an inadequate lunch, or no afternoon tea, by the time they arrive home, the person's blood sugar is likely to be through the floor, something that makes most people feel like they could eat their arm off. Instead of that, they simply polish off way too many cheese and crackers. If your need is physical and fueled by low blood sugar, then it is one physical pattern we need to address.

But what could be an example of the emotional drive to eat? A certain one is eating when you can't possibly be hungry. Most of us know, of course, that eating a whole pint of ice cream after dinner is not only not good for our health but it usually doesn't make us feel good by the time we have finished. Although you've eaten dinner, and on a physical level can't be hungry, you might still feel like you are. Perhaps, you're in the habit of eating after dinner every evening, and every evening you go to bed feeling uncomfortable and lousy and berating yourself. Lying there in discomfort, you pledge that you won't overeat again tomorrow night. And in the morning you stand by your pledge. You eat very well all day, you don't snack before dinner—even though you feel like it—you eat your dinner, and then, not long after, you start thinking about ice cream. The argument begins in your head... "I'll just have one bite. Only one. Not the whole carton. I know I said I wouldn't. But I really feel like it. What's one bite?" Something inside you knows that if you start, you won't stop. But still you start. You eat one, then two, and, before you know it, you are no longer thinking. And then the ice cream is gone. You've done it again. And then the self-loathing kicks in. You are bloated and uncomfortable, and you hate yourself. The situation seems hopeless. After nights, weeks, or even years of discomfort, you feel as if you will never be able to stop eating, and you feel as if you will never be able to lose any of your body fat. You tell yourself you have no discipline, but you need to remember that all you are doing is meeting an emotional need. Trouble is, many people are unaware of how they really feel or would prefer to deny the anger or sadness (for example) that is just below the surface. Their perception is, that it is 'safer' to not acknowledge it. We are governed by how we feel and our every drive is for survival.

We will explore emotions in detail later in this book. In this chapter, I simply wanted to show you a number of different scenarios through which excess calorie intake, no matter what the cause, can be the piece of your weight loss puzzle that needs the most attention. I also wanted to open you up to the idea that emotions may be at the heart of why you over-eat, so the emotions piece of your puzzle may also be highlighted.

Taking in too many calories is not the only reason some people cannot lose weight. Indeed, some people eat beautifully from a calorie perspective and exercise regularly, yet their body doesn't seem to change. On a physical level, this may be due to a variety of body systems, such as the production of stress hormones, the balance of sex hormones, liver function, colonic gut bacteria profiles, thyroid function, insulin, leptin hormone levels, exercise methods, alkalinity, and the nervous system. Any or all of these systems can play a role when people do all they can for little or no reward. The messages in this book do not deny that willpower has a place. Of course it does. My concern is that for people attempting to lose weight, it has been their backstop of blame. They can see no other reason other than a lack of willpower for what they classify as their failure to achieve a smaller body. But it's important to remember that we are geared for survival, and the hormonal systems outlined above know that better than any ounce of so-called will-power you can muster. If your body believes that your life is in danger, it will act accordingly; and sometimes that means fat storage, despite your best efforts. This will all make sense as you see how the pieces of your puzzle fit together.

For some, eating less is as simple as making the decision. That's it. No more overeating. They make the decision and follow through with great eating behaviors, and excess body fat is never an issue for them again. They may simply change their minds and begin to take good care of themselves, with outstanding nutrition and regular movement. For others, however, it doesn't feel as simple as making a decision. They know they "should" make a change, but it feels too hard or as if they've already "tried" everything. Some people feel that they make an effort every day and are never rewarded. So, are calories one of the pieces of your weight loss puzzle that needs attention?

SOLUTIONS FOR OVEREATING AND TOO MANY CALORIES

If the calories piece of your weight loss puzzle has been highlighted, whether at this stage you think it's caused by purely physical or emotional needs, or a combination of both, consider implementing the tips below.

- Serve dinner on a smaller plate.
- Eat two fist sizes of food (concentrated food

such as protein and/or starch) as well as plenty of greens with a high water content for most of your main meals. Snacks can be up to the size of one fist.

- Do not weigh food.

- Do not ever weigh yourself; you simply weigh your self-esteem and set yourself up to feel stressed and/or miserable over the day if you start your day this way. You know by the way your clothes fit you if your size is decreasing. Start to focus on how you feel, and work on feeling better and healthier rather than weighing less.

- Get some discipline around your thoughts. You are more likely to make poor food choices when you are (silently) saying mean things to yourself.

- Eat slowly.

- Chew each mouthful a minimum of twenty times.

- Chew each mouthful and swallow before you put the next mouthful in.

- Eat regularly; don't get ravenous so you feel like you want to eat your arm off.

- When you are first making changes, set

short-term targets for yourself. If you eat
takeout most days, you could try starting
with "I am not going to eat any takeout
until Friday, and then I can have whatever
I like." Or if you don't usually eat many
vegetables, commit yourself to eating vegetables for six out of the next seven nights.
Perhaps you drink too much sugar because
of the wine or soda you consume? In that
case, decide to drink these beverages only
on Friday or Saturday, rather than every
night. It is also important to reflect on how
you feel when you follow through with
what you say you will do. Commend yourself—but not with a food or drink reward.
Look yourself in the eye and tell yourself
you are proud of yourself. You may feel a
trifle foolish at first, but persevere until you
can hold your own gaze as you say the kind
words to yourself.

- Allow some short-term targets to stretch
  beyond a week to two weeks.

Remind yourself that you keep your word
in your commitments to other people. So it's
time to show yourself you truly care about
yourself and keep your word for these short

bursts of time. As you explore the other factors involved in body fat in this book, you will begin to see there is much you can do to change your desire for food in the first place.

Stress
Hormones
Puzzle Piece 2

Your adrenal glands are two very precious, walnut-sized glands that sit just on top of your kidneys. They may be small in stature, but the power they pack when they are working optimally is an energetic gift to us all. The adrenal glands produce many hormones, two of which are your stress hormones, namely adrenaline and cortisol.

Adrenaline is your short-term stress hormone. It is your acute stress hormone, the one that's produced when you get a fright. If someone suddenly runs into the room and startles you and you jump, that feeling that most of us know very well is caused by adrenalin. Adrenaline is designed to get you out of danger—and get you out of danger fast. Historically, we made adrenaline when our life was being threatened, and our response, fueled by adrenalin, was typically physical. A tiger might have suddenly jumped out of the jungle at us or perhaps a member of another tribe came running with a spear. In that moment, you made adrenaline to get out of danger. Adrenaline promotes what is known as the "fight or flight" response. When activated, the typically excellent blood supply to your digestive system is diverted away from your digestive system to your periphery, to your arms and your legs. This is necessary because you need a powerful blood supply to your arms and legs to get you out of danger. You also need fuel to give them the necessary energy; the most readily available fuel is glucose, often referred to as sugar (a carbohydrate). Your liver and your muscles store glucose in the form of glycogen, and adrenaline communicates to your liver and your muscles that energy is required. They then convert glycogen back into glucose and dump this glucose into your blood. Your blood sugar subsequently shoots up, ready to fuel your self-defense or your escape.

This cascade of events—and the biochemical changes that result—allows you to escape from danger in a very active way. Regardless of the outcome, regardless of whether you win that challenge or not (you escape, die, or win the fight), this stress, the threat to your life, and the need for adrenaline is over very quickly. The trouble is that for many of us in the modern world, it is more often psychological stress that drives us to make adrenalin. And so although our life may not literally be threatened, this hormone still communicates to every cell of our body that our life is indeed at risk.

Psychological stress can come in many forms. It may be that you return from a two-week holiday to find 800 new emails in your inbox, and you wonder when on earth you're going to find the time to deal with those. It may be that your landline rings and, while you take that call, your mobile rings, and you feel that you can barely finish one conversation before demands begin to start another. It could be that you set your alarm for the morning, you press snooze... you keep pressing snooze and suddenly you sit bolt upright in bed and realize you're running late. You may still have to iron clothes, prepare lunches, deliver little people to school and, because you're leaving later than usual, you get stuck in traffic. Meanwhile, your mobile phone starts ringing with people at the office wondering where you are as you are supposed to be in a meeting, but you are stuck in the middle of rush hour traffic, and your brain has gone into overdrive with the enormity of your morning. And you've only been up for an hour!

When you finally burst through the doors at work, all you can think about is how much you want a coffee. So all morning you've been making adrenalin, and now you are going to make even more adrenalin, as caffeine promotes its production. All you actually want from the "coffee" at this point in your day is a little breathing space. The reasons we crave a hot drink may vary, but often it's just to catch our breath. In those coffee break moments, there is a bubble around us, and we are silently communicating, "Don't you dare come near me for the next three minutes!"

One important difference between the past and modern day is that the biochemical changes generated by adrenalin, such as sugar being dumped into your blood to get you out of danger, serve a useful purpose while you are physically fighting or fleeing.

If you're sitting on your bottom at your desk in front of a computer and sugar is being dumped into your blood, you make insulin to deal with that elevation in blood sugar. And insulin is one of our primary fat storage hormones, as you will see in later chapters.

How coffee can make you fat

Caffeine acts on your adrenal glands by stimulating the production of adrenalin. When adrenaline is released, your blood sugar elevates to provide more energy, your blood pressure and pulse rate rise to provide more oxygen to the muscles, which tense in preparation for action. Your pupils also dilate to see more in less light, your immune function stops firing as, from the body's perspective, fighting infection is not essential at this unsafe point in time. Blood is diverted away from digestion, and reproductive functions are downregulated since they use a lot of energy and are not necessary for our immediate survival, given the impending threat. Plus, your body does not believe it is "safe" to bring a baby into what your body perceives is an unsafe world. Not when your stress hormones are telling your body that your life is in danger (adrenalin) or that there is no more food left in the world (cortisol)!

Whether your adrenaline production is the result of real or perceived stress, or simply the result of your caffeine intake, caffeine, via stress hormones and coupled with the response of your nervous system (explored later in detail), can either lead you to slenderness or fat storage, because insulin—the fat storage hormone—will firstly convert unused glucose from your blood into glycogen and store it in your muscles and what is left over will be converted into body fat. Let me explain this with the story of a client I'll call Anne. This strikingly slim and physically beautiful woman had an appointment to see me. I did what I do with every client, and asked how I could help her and what she would like to get out of our session. Anne apologized for what she thought would sound vain and said that she had gained seven pounds recently and was seeing me because nothing in her diet or activity level had changed and could be attributed to the weight gain. She was concerned that she may be perimenopausal even though her periods had not changed. She said some of her friends had gained weight during perimenopause, and she was here because she was concerned that those seven pounds would become twenty before she knew it, if she didn't get to the bottom of why her body had changed. I admired Anne's attitude and her desire to understand her body better. We discussed the many facets of her life, emotional and physical, and when it came time to talk about her food, her diet was truly amazing with regards to all of my benchmarks of eating a diet based on fresh foods. People like me have numerous strategies (as you will see) that we can apply to assist someone in their quest for fat loss; from a food perspective this lady was already living by all the tricks of my trade. When it came time to talk about her liquid intake, she politely informed me that she had one glass of red wine four times per week and that she had done this with her husband for years. And then I asked if she drank coffee. Anne's eyes lit up. She replied that, yes, she loved it, but acknowledged, on reflection, that her caffeine intake *was* something that had changed. She had always had a coffee before breakfast every day for most of her adult life, and that was the only caffeine she consumed all day. But for the past three to four months, she had begun to have up to four coffees per day, but she didn't know why. She just had. When my eyes lit up back at her, she quickly justified her intake by saying, "But they are all black coffees, so there are no calories in them." She drank them all at her desk. She had never exercised, and I could see she had very little muscle mass. Her fat had gone on around her tummy.

Anne could see from the look on my face where I was about to go and, before I'd even spoken, she said "Please don't take them from me." I wanted her to see how emotionally attached she was so I didn't interrupt her. Eventually, I said that I believed it was the coffee that had led her to gain her seven pounds, and she cried. She told me it was impossible, and she kept coming back to the calorie reasoning. She virtually had a tantrum in my office. I gently tried to lead her to the truth that actually it's only a drink, yet she behaved as if her four daily coffees held the meaning of life for her. I then went on to explain the mechanism I outlined above involving caffeine, adrenalin, elevated blood sugar, and subsequent insulin production. I told her that I wasn't even asking her to give up caffeine entirely. My clients will tell you that, when it is warranted, I often ask them to give up caffeine completely for four weeks. They are often shocked by how much more energy they have without caffeine in their lives. I simply wanted this client to go back to her one cup a day before breakfast, a coffee prepared with love by her husband. Anne agreed to make this change for four weeks, even though she couldn't imagine anything being more powerful than calories in fat creation and couldn't see how this plan could possibly work. I did nothing else for this woman. Not one other change to her dietary intake and, four weeks later, she burst through my door telling me she had lost nine pounds in four weeks. She had only gained seven in the first place. I have never weighed a client nor will I ever weigh a client. My theory was that Anne's weight gain was the result of the perception of her nervous system, rather than the result of too many calories. Her subsequent weight loss was, in my opinion, extremely fast, but my point in sharing this story with you is to demonstrate caffeine's power to signal what is, for some, fat storage. Granted, this will not happen for everyone. It is significantly dependent on, as I mentioned earlier, the balance of your nervous system (discussed in detail in later sections).

So consider your caffeine habits and get honest with yourself about how it affects you. Does it dull your appetite and so unconsciously you grab a coffee instead of eating? This is especially true for many women at lunchtime. Does it make your heart race, give you the shakes, or loosen your bowels? Does it elevate your blood pressure? Or does it nourish your soul with no ill effect whatsoever? You know yourself better than anyone. Act on what you know is true for you.

Think about all of these mechanisms. So many of us run on adrenalin. Moment to moment, day to day, it's like a light switch has gone on, and it hasn't entirely switched off for a really long time. And it doesn't have to be traumatic stress and shocking situations that drive this process in us. It can simply be the pace at which we live our lives; the juggling act that leads so many people I meet to say that they want more "balance" in their lives. Some people even seek the feeling adrenaline gives them, and they only feel like they are living when adrenaline is pumping through their veins.

The human body is incredibly resilient, and although we were not designed to withstand long-term stress (due to the way we're designed, we are healthier when it is short-lived), many bodies appear to tolerate, as opposed to thrive on, years and years of living on adrenaline. Part of the challenge, however, is that once your body perceives that the stress has become long-term, your dominant stress hormone begins to change.

CORTISOL—FRIEND OR WORST NIGHTMARE

Cortisol is your long-term stress hormone. Historically, the only long-term stress humans had revolved around food being scarce. Long-term stress came in the form of floods, famines, and wars. During such times, a person never knew where the next meal was coming from. Today, in the Western world, our long-term stresses tend to be more along the lines of financial stress, relationship concerns, and uncertainty, or even worries, about our health—even our weight.

For so many people, their first waking thoughts involve "What will I or won't I eat today?" or "How much exercise can I get done today?"

Or, for some, the thoughts might flow like this: "Oh, my goodness, it's Wednesday, and I still haven't been to the gym, and, my gosh, it's 7:00 p.m. and there's no food at home, which means I still have to the supermarket, and if I go to the supermarket that means I won't get home until 8:30 p.m. and then I have to cook and clean up and then it will be midnight before I get to bed and I have to get up at a good time to get to work early in the morning, but I'm going to a party in three weeks and I really wanted to fit into my favorite red dress and that's not going to happen because I haven't been to the gym all week and I am still not going to go tonight because otherwise I won't get any sleep and get to work on time to do everything I have to do… " and on and on and on it goes. So many people live like this most days of their life. When it happens day after day it can easily lead to a chronic pattern of stress response, hence increased cortisol output, which in turn can lead to a change in your metabolism.

It is important to understand how cortisol works, as it can be your friend or one of your worst nightmares! When made at optimum amounts, cortisol does numerous wonderful things for your health. It is one of the body's primary anti-inflammatory mediators, meaning that wherever there is inflammation in the body, cortisol, having been converted into cortisone, dampens down the effect of that inflammation and stops your body from feeling stiff, rigid, or in pain. Many people, for example, will describe the feeling that they have suddenly aged as they come out of difficult times. In the right amount, cortisol is not only an anti-inflammatory, it also buffers the effect of insulin, meaning that optimum amounts help you continue to burn body fat for energy while also maintaining stable—as opposed to rapidly fluctuating—blood sugar levels.

Cortisol levels change over the day. The right amount assists you with various bodily functions throughout the course of the day. Cortisol is designed to be high in the morning and, for the purpose of this discussion, let's say that 25 units at around 6:00 am are ideal. Cortisol is one of the mechanisms that wakes you up in the morning and helps you bounce out of bed full of energy and vitality. By midday, optimum cortisol will sit at around 15 units, and, by 6:00 pm, levels will ideally be at around four units. By 10:00 pm in the evening, optimum cortisol levels are around two units, a level at which they are designed to stay until around 2:00 am when they slowly and very steadily begin to rise again.

The following illustration shows this graphically. It is true what your mother told you, that one hour of sleep before midnight is worth two after, because cortisol starts to rise around 2:00 am and the waking up process gradually begins. Do you ever wake up around 2:00 am? Continue reading, for it may be related to your adrenal glands, your liver... or both!

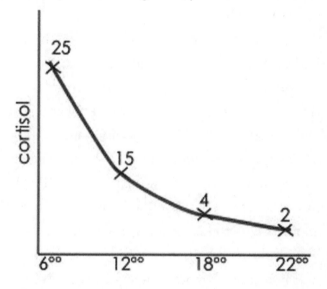

The Optimal Cortisol Profile: *Cortisol is nice and high in the morning and falls away again by the evening.*

As a stress response continues, the effect on the body begins to change. In the early stages of stress, one of the first challenges cortisol presents is that the evening level of the hormone starts to spike again rather than continuing to decrease. At this stage, you still make optimum levels in the morning and are able to bounce out of bed and get on with your day with reasonable energy, but evening levels are creeping up. This is one mechanism through which good sleeping patterns can be challenged.

When cortisol levels become elevated above optimal, other changes in body chemistry begin to unfold. It has been suggested that elevated cortisol is the one common thread behind what we have come to describe as metabolic syndrome; that is elevated blood pressure, elevated cholesterol, and insulin resistance, the latter condition being a warning sign that if nothing changes in the near future, Type 2 diabetes is a likely consequence. If we remember that we are completely geared for survival and that cortisol tells every cell of your body that food is scarce, another of its roles is to slow down your metabolic rate. A slower metabolism leads you to burn body fat for energy far more slowly then you have in the past, as cortisol is designed to make sure that you survive this perceived period of famine.

Cortisol is "catabolic," meaning that it breaks protein down into its building blocks, known as amino acids. Your muscles are made from proteins, and cortisol signals them to break down, as the body's perception is that fuel is needed. Additional amino acids are also needed in the blood to help repair tissues (even though you may be simply sitting on your bottom in front of the television, with your financial or relationship concerns mulling around your head!). The amino acids released as a result of the catabolic signaling of cortisol can be converted, through a process called "gluconeogenesis," back into glucose (sugar), which your body thinks may be useful to assist you in your stress. Yet if you're not active, this increase in blood glucose will not be utilized, and insulin will have to be secreted to return blood glucose levels to normal by returning the glucose in the blood to storage. Remember that glucose is stored as glycogen in the muscles and the liver.

But over time, the catabolic signaling of cortisol itself may have broken some of your muscles down, so now there is less space for glucose storage. As a result, some of the blood glucose returns to the remaining muscles while the leftovers are converted into body fat. Keeping the glucose level of the blood within the normal, safe range is of more importance to your body than whether you have wobbly bits around your middle! Essentially, too much cortisol can make you fat through dysregulated blood sugar metabolism, not just fat metabolism itself. This is also the process through which long-term stress can lead to Type 2 diabetes.

Because cortisol is produced when the stress in

your life has been going on for a while, your body (not knowing any better) thinks there is no more food left in your world, and it instinctively knows that it has a greater chance of survival if it holds on to some extra body fat. In modern times, when, for health reasons or vanity (or both), many people understand the importance of not carrying too much body fat, cortisol can provide a potential challenge to someone who believes that eating less is their only solution to body fat loss.

UNDERSTANDING THE CORTISOL PROBLEM

if cortisol tells every cell of your body that food is scarce, and your metabolism slows down as a result, and you continue to eat and exercise in the same way you always have, your clothes will slowly get tighter. It doesn't matter how amazingly you eat. With cortisol telling every cell in your body to store fat, it is very difficult, if not impossible, to decrease body fat until the cortisol issue is resolved. We must get to the heart of the stress and either change the situation or change the perception.

Cortisol has a very distinct fat deposition pattern. You typically lay it on around your tummy, and, once again, the reason for fat placement here is governed by the body's quest for survival. If food suddenly ran out, your major organs have very easy access to fat that will keep you alive. You also tend to lay fat down on the back of the arms, and you grow what I lovingly call a back veranda. To reiterate this important point: what do most people do when they notice that their clothes are getting tighter? They go on a diet, and, when you go on a diet, do you tend to eat more or less? You typically eat less (although some audience members call out "more" when I ask them this question at a seminar!), and in doing so you reaffirm to your body that food is scarce. But food is not scarce. It is abundant for you. If you want a chocolate bar at 3:00 a.m., you can get one. Eating less on your diet confirms to your body what it perceives to be true and that slows your metabolism even further.

Another challenge you face with elevated cortisol coursing through your body is that, since your body thinks that food is scarce, any time you see food, it's very easy to overeat, no matter how firmly you intend to eat only three crackers when you get home from work! If that packet of crackers is open and in front of you, cortisol will scream at every cell of your body, "You are so lucky! There's food there! Eat it!" and somehow, before you know it, the whole box of crackers is gone. Please don't get me wrong... I am not saying that self-discipline and willpower have no place. My intention is simply to point out that we have very ancient hormonal mechanisms in action inside our bodies that believe they know better than you when it comes to your survival. Your body can be your biggest teacher if you learn how to decipher the messages it is communicating to you. And extra body fat is sometimes simply a vehicle of communication.

SILENT STRESS

what about when the stress is silent? You might not be a drama queen running around, arms flailing all over the place, screeching "I'm so stressed, I'm so stressed!" You may be a very private person and keep things mostly to yourself. You may be so private with your fears and concerns, only presenting a happy face to the world, that you don't even realize that you're worried about things or that may have been in a stressed state for a very long time.

When you feel grateful for the life you have, it's very easy to feel guilty if you complain about anything. A common internal phrase will be, "There are so many people worse off than me." This thought immediately makes you feel guilty and you stop focusing on your source of stress. Trouble is, although there *are* people worse off than you in this world, the minute you feel guilty, you change your focus so you don't ever get the opportunity to truly identify what is bothering you and, more importantly, why.

These "whys" are explored in detail in the emotions section of the book. For now, I'll share a common example, one that involves keeping the peace, to help you determine if cortisol, from an emotional source, is a likely piece we need to solve in your weight loss puzzle.

Basic psychology teaches us that humans will do more to avoid pain than they will ever do to experience pleasure. Some people I meet will do anything, for example, to keep the peace and avoid conflict. Inwardly they become highly strung because they are always walking on eggshells around others, usually their intimate partner. Hello, silent stress hormone production! Others avoid feeling emotional pain by eating too much or making other poor food choices; perhaps by drinking bucket loads of wine or chain-smoking cigarettes. Alternatively, some people might write in a journal, go for a walk, a run, or a swim, while others will phone a friend and chat to deal with emotional pain. And all of these activities may take place with no conscious understanding of why.

WORRYING CAN MAKE YOU FAT

You think you want to lose weight more than anything? You think you would do anything to be slimmer? You probably already have all of the information you need to do this. So what's stopping you? Or what stops you once you've started?

Every day of my working life, I meet people who eat too much. They know they do, but they can't seem to stop. Sometimes it is nutritious food, sometimes it's not, but, whatever the case, they know they would be much better off if they ate less.

Often these people are seeing me because they want to lose weight and they are precious, intelligent people who don't understand why they do what they do. These people know what to eat and what not to eat to lose weight, yet they don't do it, even though they truly believe that they are desperate to lose weight.

There is a really big difference between eating two squares of chocolate and eating the entire block, between one cookie with a cup of tea in the evening and eating a dozen. We all know that eating too much makes us feel full and uncomfortable, but, worse, it usually drives us to say very unkind things to ourselves such as "I'm so useless, I have no willpower," and makes us go to bed feeling guilty and sad and believing we will never be able to change. That belief that things are permanent is very destructive.

So what might be going on for someone who, even with good intentions, just can't stop eating? Besides elevated cortisol caused by long-term stress, there may be other biochemical factors involved such as low progesterone, poor thyroid function, or blood sugar that surges and plummets. There are also likely to be emotional factors and core beliefs they probably aren't even aware of.

One of the most wonderful and helpful statements my mother ever said to me was, "Don't worry about something until it's a problem." If it becomes a problem, then you can face it, but worrying about something that truly may never happen only serves to hurt you. As we now know, stress, whether it is real or perceived, may promote the production of excess cortisol! The ripple effect of a worry can very slowly and subtly change your metabolism to one of fat storage and a headspace of sadness and withdrawal. And it's the chemical signals of your body that are driving this. The beautiful, old piece of wisdom called "The Serenity Prayer" is useful to remember and act on, especially if you are a worrier:

> *God, grant me the serenity to accept the things*
> *I cannot change,*
> *Courage to change the things I can,*
> *And the wisdom to know the difference.*

The next biochemical stage of stress that can occur, especially if the stress has been prolonged, may involve cortisol falling low. If you have had a high level of cortisol output for many, many years, your adrenal glands may not be able to stand the tension. They were never designed to sustain this kind of output and so they crash. In general terms, you "burnout." In more recent times, this has become known as adrenal fatigue, because the major symptom is a deep and unrelenting fatigue.

Cortisol is supposed to be high in the morning, and ideal amounts help you bounce out of bed. It plays a role in how vital you feel and helps the body combat any inflammatory processes that want to kick in. Stiffness is a key symptom of adrenal fatigue. For those with chronic stress, morning cortisol levels tend to be low, and, if twenty-five units is the ideal, with adrenal stress you may only get to ten units. It can be very difficult to get out of bed with such low levels. By midafternoon, it will be at an all-time low, and you feel you need something sweet, something containing caffeine, or a nap to get you through your afternoon (this can also be the result of low blood sugar, which is covered in detail in the insulin chapter, or poor thyroid function, which is also explored in a later chapter). For an adrenally fatigued person, cortisol is nice and low in the evenings, but if you don't go to bed before 10:00 p.m., you will typically get a second wind, and it will be much harder for you to fall asleep if you're still up at midnight. The following graph illustrates this.

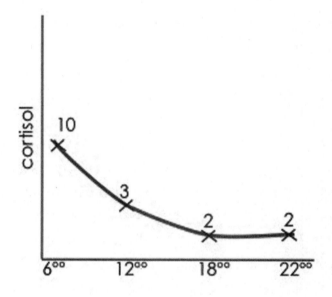

A typical cortisol profile of an adrenally fatigued person:
Note particularly, the low waking cortisol and low midday reading.

When cortisol drops low, it is likely that prior to this it was high (although not always), and body fat may have increased during this time. But just because it is low does not mean easy access to body fat burning due to cortisol's relationship to insulin, described earlier.

Additionally, the fatigue you feel with this bio-chemical picture may make exercise the least appealing thing on the planet to you. You actually feel worse after exercise when you are adrenally fatigued, whereas exercise typically energizes us. Frustration mounts because you believe that exercising and eating less are the only solutions to weight loss, yet you can't bring yourself to do either despite every good intention. Every time you eat something sweet, you eat too much, or another month goes past without much movement. When you reflect on this, you feel guilty, you might say mean things to yourself—and you may silently lose hope. You think "who cares?" now whenever you feel like eating something that won't really nourish you, and the not-so-great eating continues, especially an excess consumption of carbohydrates as you desperately search for energy. Your clothes keep getting tighter and this just adds to your stress. The vicious cycle is self-perpetuating.

Humans were never designed to sustain long-term stress, and our individual bodies cope with it in different ways. For some, adrenaline remains the dominant stress hormone all of their lives, while others may flip over into a more cortisol-dominant stress response. If the stress response doesn't truly switch off, there is the potential that the adrenals will eventually crash, and cortisol output is no longer optimum or elevated. It will be negligible. At its extreme, this is a condition called Addison's disease, yet if a person's cortisol level is extremely low but still falls just inside the "normal' range," that person will be told that they are fine. They feel lousy but all the tests they have always come back "normal." They feel anything but normal, and people who know and love them will often comment that they are a shell of their former selves.

Cortisol can also be rather sinister in that it can interfere with your steroid (sex) hormone metabolism (explained in the next chapter, this is truly fascinating), your sleep patterns via its interference with melatonin, and also your mood via serotonin. Let's look at them.

THE SEROTONIN-MELATONIN SEESAW

Is this your typical day? Healthy breakfast, mid-morning coffee, salad or sandwich for lunch… with probably something sweet to follow lunch but other than that, you are quite proud of yourself when you reflect on your food consumption so far for the day.

But I predict that many of you then fall into one of three categories. Do you:

1. Hit midafternoon and eat anything and

everything in sight and then spend the rest of the day berating yourself after such a great start?

2. Get so busy during the afternoon that food does not enter your head until you arrive home and a glass of white wine and possibly some cheese and crackers allows you to let out a sigh of relief that the day is winding down?

3. Or is it neither of the above and the free-for-all starts after dinner, when you find yourself standing in front of the fridge or pantry saying to yourself "I want something. I don't know what it is that I want but I want something. And maybe it's in here!"

Perhaps all three of these scenarios apply to you! Never fear, a new understanding is near.

Options 1 and 2 are explored in later chapters (mostly as part of the insulin puzzle piece) and are primarily about blood glucose. Option 3 describes "Captain Serotonin." Serotonin is our happy, calm, content hormone. It is the hormone that helps us feel like there is nothing for which we want in this world. It makes us very content with our lot in life. Melatonin is our sleep hormone and is responsible for sending us to, and keeping us, asleep. These hormones work antagonistically. That is, one goes up, the other goes down.

In our bodies we have what are called circadian rhythms, which govern a multitude of hormonal processes. These rhythms, coupled with fading sunlight, allow melatonin to rise, which, in turn, means serotonin must fall.

When a hormone that makes you feel happy, calm, and content decreases, it can create a noticeable sinking feeling, a distinct change in mood even though nothing in the external world has changed. Five minutes before, you felt fine, yet now there is this nagging feeling that you want something. There is a chance that a relatively lower level of serotonin as evening falls is partly why couples have conversations about "big ticket items" at this time of day. Our chemistry makes us feel like we want something and our brain tries to label what that might be. We usually don't find ourselves waking up and announcing that we absolutely must renovate the bathroom immediately! We keep those proclamations for evening. Serotonin has much to answer for.

Humans instinctively know that carbohydrate-rich foods promote serotonin production, which is partly why when the "I want something" syndrome hits, we head for the pantry. We hope what we want is in there. Usually, though, guilt is all we find.

Mornings can also prove a challenge for someone in this pattern. Melatonin is destroyed by sunlight, which is partly why when we go outside and exercise in the morning we tend to feel great all day. The melatonin plummets when the retina of our eyes is exposed to light and, as a result, our serotonin surges. On a day where you get up and expose your eyes to sunlight, with that hormonal profile, we can cope with anything. The flip side, though, is not so appealing. If we've gone to bed after midnight, not slept well, or both, we may not want to rise with the sun as we don't feel rested. If we just wander out of bed sometime during the morning, our melatonin slowly seeps away, and our serotonin slowly rises. On such a day, we feel like we need a few coffees to get ourselves going.

If this tale is ringing true for you, and the carb-fest in the evening feels out of control, the solution is not initially—or always—purely dietary.

Step one is to start getting up at the same time each morning and going outside and moving. Or at least open the curtains and recognize a new day has dawned. Welcome the day with tai chi, a walk, or a run, whatever floats your boat. Commit to doing this for four weeks, every day, and observe if your evening carbohydrate cravings settle. Your serotonin will love you for it.

As you can see, cortisol plays many roles in our body, and optimal levels are essential for us to be able to access body fat to burn it, to feel content, have good energy, and keep inflammation and pain at bay. Is cortisol one of the factors you must address to solve your weight loss puzzle?

How high your level of stress is and how you feel your body copes with it will influence the steps you take after reading this section. The first section of solutions is general, and I can confidently say that virtually everyone will benefit from applying them.

The herbs used for adrenal support are beautiful, however it is best to check with a qualified medical herbalist to find out about herbs that will meet your specific needs. I have made comments beside most of the herbs about their applications.

If you have identified that you are adrenally fatigued and beyond exhausted on a daily basis, your adrenal support is listed separately.

As you can already see, our perceptions play an enormous role in whether we are stressed or not. Sometimes it may be trauma in the past that takes a toll on your body. Even though you know in your mind you have dealt with it or moved on, your unconscious mind still wrestles with it. Or stress can be from comparatively "little" things. It is as if you have an itch that somehow gets scratched by your beloved, your children, your boss, or by random people. Our bodies go through everything with us, and despite our minds consciously moving on, sometimes our bodies are stuck in the past. If this rings true for you, I suggest you read this entire book before you set about "solving" anything. After your first full read, return to each section and construct your plan. Even more deeply, I hope that the messages on these pages will allow you to open yourself up to a new perspective on health, on food, on movement, on life, on feeling, on your beliefs, and, so importantly, on how safe you feel in this world. There are some wonderful methods through which you can help shift your body and your emotions when you feel like you have cognitively processed the living daylights out of your stress, yet it still remains a challenge or your weight is still stuck. These are listed below.

HOW YOUR NERVOUS SYSTEM AFFECTS YOUR HEALTH

At the heart of all of my strategies to support you adrenally is the desire for you to rest and to rest well, in a restorative and revitalizing way. Rest must follow action for us to have optimal health and excellent fat burning, and very few of us these days truly rest, although we might believe we do. A part of our nervous system called the parasympathetic nervous system (PNS) is active when we truly rest. This is the "rest and repair" arm of our nervous system, but it can be dominated by the opposite arm of the nervous system, the sympathetic nervous system (SNS). This is described in more detail in a later chapter. For now, all you need to know is that if you do not lose weight from high-intensity exercise, it is likely that your sympathetic nervous system is dominant. If you do shift weight from this type of exercise, then your nervous system is likely to be well-balanced. Both the PNS and the SNS are part of the autonomic nervous system (ANS).

THE IMPORTANCE OF BREATHING WELL

The other reason for this relatively brief section about the nervous system here is to make you aware of the cornerstone of all my adrenal support solutions and, just as importantly, explain *why* I will insist on this if you take nothing else away from this book. It has nothing to do with food, and it is absolutely free to everyone. It is called breathing, and it is the key to shifting our chemistry from fat storage to fat burning. How is this possible?

The role of the ANS is to perceive the internal

environment and, after processing the information in the central nervous system (CNS), regulate the function of your internal environment. The name "autonomic" implies that it is independent of the conscious mind. Think about a family of ducks and their newborn ducklings. Just like ducklings, the autonomic nervous system will always follow the leader, and the breath is the *only* part of the autonomic nervous system that can be controlled consciously. Your breath leads. Your body follows. Breathing dominates your autonomic nervous system, and because we breathe 5,000 to 30,000 times a day—or two to five hundred million times in your lifetime—it has the potential to influence you positively or negatively in many ways.

Nothing communicates to every cell of your body that you are safe better than your breath. If you breathe in a shallow way, with short, sharp inhalations and exhalations, then you communicate to your body that your life is in danger. You have just learnt about the cascade of hormonal events that follow such alarm and the role these hormones play in switching fat burning on or off. How your breathe is also a fast track to the symptoms of anxiety and, potentially, panic attacks, regardless of what led you to breathe in a shallow way in the first place, whether it was an event, a deadline, the perception of pressure and the consequent "need" to rush, or the lifetime habit of your nervous system. Long, slow breathing that moves your diaphragm, communicates the opposite message to your body—that you are very safe. Nothing downregulates the production of fat storage stress hormones more powerfully.

So, solution number one is to practice diaphragmatic breathing, making sure your tummy moves in and out as you breathe, as opposed to your upper chest. Schedule it at first until it becomes your new way of breathing (unless you literally do need to escape from danger such as slamming your foot on the brake if another car suddenly drives out in front of you!). Make appointments with yourself to breathe. If it is peaceful each morning while you boil the kettle for the first time that day (to make your hot water with lemon of course!), instead of racing around and doing eighty jobs while the kettle boils, stand in your kitchen and breathe.

Link breathing well to a daily routine, such as boiling the kettle or having a shower, so that it quickly becomes a habit. Do it numerous times over the course of your day. Book a meeting into your diary each afternoon at 3:00 pm. If you work at a computer, have it pop up on the screen that it is time for your meeting with yourself to do twenty long, slow breaths. We keep appointments with other people, so be sure to keep the appointments you make with yourself. Take part in movement that facilitates a focus on the breath such as tai chi, qi gong, yoga, or walking quietly in nature. Pilates can also be useful, but I have found that it is highly dependent on your attitude while you are doing the session and also to some degree on the attitude of the instructor. This approach is partly about stilling the stories that we constantly bark on about in our mind.

THE IMPORTANCE OF LAUGHTER

Another free and powerful tool is laughter. If we see life as tough, full of hard work, pain, and drudgery, it will be precisely that. Humans have the ability to only see their perspective in the world, rather than the world as it truly is. We see the world through filters, yet we don't know they are there. I am not denying that life can be tough at times or that being honest with ourselves if we do feel down and out about life is not a good thing. The problem comes when we see the world this way and believe that it will never be any different. For then it won't be.

Think about it. A belief in the permanence of doom is dangerous for every hormonal signal in your body. Do your absolute best to shift your thinking to see life as an adventure, a journey and a gift, full of opportunity, a process through which we can contribute. Some of the greatest, most moving stories I have ever heard have involved someone turning a horrific hardship into their greatest opportunity. Keep this in mind.

SOLUTIONS FOR ADRENAL SUPPORT

- Schedule and commit to regular breathing exercises. It can literally change your life. And I do not say that lightly.

- Practice yoga, Pilates, tai chi, or qigong a minimum of twice a week for four weeks. Develop a daily practice for outstanding results.

- Spend five minutes daily focusing on and giving voice to all the aspects of your life for which you are grateful; you can't be stressed when you feel grateful.

- With the guidance of an herbalist, take some adrenal support herbs. I am not associated with any brands of supplements, but when I have good reason to favor one I will mention it. When it comes to herbs, nothing compares to Mediherb, an Australian-based company (products available internationally) with the highest of standards. I mostly use liquid tinctures and, at times, the tablet combinations. The majority of these adrenal herbs are adaptogens, meaning they help the body adapt to stress by fine tuning the stress response. They include:

- o Withania, for the worriers

- o Rhodiola, for the drama queens or occasionally for the worriers

- o Siberian Ginseng, for the fatigued feminine

- o Panex Ginseng; for the utterly fatigued and for short-term use only

- o Licorice, especially if your blood pressure is on the low end of normal

- o Dandelion leaves, especially if you retain fluid

- The adrenals also love vitamin B and vitamin C, and for adrenal   support I usually supplement both: the B's in the form of a multi vitamin or a straight B complex, plus 4-5 grams per day of vitamin C, preferably in powered form with added calcium and magnesium. If you are on an oral contraceptive pill, stick to 2 grams of vitamin C per day.

- Just as important, if not the *most* important aspect of supporting adrenal function for a balanced and appropriate stress hormone response, is the application of the emotional health strategies (explored in the emotions chapter) and breathing. I know breathing sounds too simple to make a difference but diaphragmatic breathing (making your tummy move in and out as you breathe, as opposed to your upper chest) can literally change your life. And I do not say that lightly.

Adrenal fatigue supplementation

for people with deep, deep fatigue, I almost always use the following herbal tonic that contains:

- Panex ginseng

- Licorice

- Dandelion leaves

- Astragalus

- One other herb depending on what else is going on for the individual (a liver herb or a reproductive herb are typical)

I will also sometimes use a range of supplements

from the United States created by Dr. James Wilson specifically for adrenal fatigue. I have had countless clients take this range of supplements for three months and have their energy and vitality return to great levels.

The restorative power of good food

although I often recommend supplements of herbs and/or nutrients for adrenal fatigue, never underestimate the healing and restorative power of food the way it comes in nature. Taking supplements is not a reason to eat a poor quality, low-nutrient diet. I simply recommend supplements where appropriate and especially to assist in the restoration of health.

Sex Hormones
Puzzle Piece 3

Sex hormones can be delicious substances that give you energy and vitality and yet they can also wreck havoc on your life. When it comes to fat burning, beautiful skin, mental clarity, a sense of calm, the ability to be patient and not make mountains out of molehills, as well as fertility, very few substances in our body impact us more than our sex hormones.

The main sex hormones we will cover in this

chapter are estrogen and progesterone, with a particular focus on their role in body shape, size, and fat burning.

CAN ESTROGEN MAKE YOU FAT?

Estrogen is a feminine hormone (although men naturally make it in small amounts), and it plays numerous important roles in the human body, including ones associated with reproduction, promoting new bone growth, and supporting cardiovascular health. The challenge with estrogen, however, occurs when there is too much of it compared to other hormones, progesterone in particular. Estrogen can also pose a problem if there is too much of one type of estrogen compared to other types of estrogen.

Estrogen is made by the ovaries of menstruating females, and small amounts are produced by fat stores and the adrenal glands. At menopause, ovarian production of hormones ceases.

The role of estrogen in the female body from a reproductive perspective is to lay down the lining of the uterus, which it does between days one and fourteen of a typical twenty-eight day reproductive cycle, with day one of the cycle being the first day of menstruation. The estrogen lays the lining of the uterus down over these first fourteen days to prepare the female body for a conception if it takes place. Estrogen prepares a menstruating female to fall pregnant every single month of her life, whether she wants to or not! Remember, our bodies are completely geared for survival, and perpetuation of the human species is an enormous part of that survival process.

As a result of the biological imperative to conceive each month, estrogen ensures there is adequate body fat, as most females will not know immediately that they have fallen pregnant. In the event that the woman is a stick figure without much body fat, it is possible that a brand new fetus may not survive. To prevent this estrogen signals fat to be laid down in typically female areas, giving women a pear-like shape to better serve the childbirth process.

Estrogen is the hormone that makes female breasts bud at the first signs of puberty, it broadens our hips, and it gives us our curves. It lays down fat on a woman's hips, bottom, and thighs, and is typically responsible for making the bottom half of a female body broader than the top half. Estrogen also, unfortunately, promotes fluid retention when it is in excess.

FLUID RETENTION

I am convinced that many women "feel" fat when really they are either bloated or retaining fluid. I have never once weighed a client and I don't encourage my clients to weigh themselves either. I do this for many reasons, but one is certainly because as hormone levels fluctuate over the month, so can the amount of fluid being retained until the hormones return to balance. Besides, when you weigh yourself, remember that all you are really doing is weighing your self-esteem. I have met thousands of women who can gain six pounds in a day, and to say that this messes with their mind is an understatement. If you get on the scales in the morning and weigh 150 pounds, and, by the evening, you weigh 156 pounds, especially if you have eaten well and done some exercise that day and even if you *haven't* eaten perfectly or exercised that day, it's easy to feel incredibly disheartened and wonder how on earth this could possibly happen.

Remember this: *it is not physically possible* to gain six pounds of body fat in a single day. The only possible cause is fluid retention. Yet even though the logical part of the female mind will know this, seeing six extra pounds on the scales over the course of just a day, or even a week, will make most women, no matter how logical, feel fat, flat, and lousy. As an aside, are you more likely to make good food choices when you feel flat? Are you likely to want to be intimate with your partner when you feel fleshy and puffy?

Usually not and then you (and they!) feel worse.

There can be numerous factors behind fluid retention, too many to go into here, but in a nutshell, fluid retention can be driven by poor lymphatic flow, mineral deficiencies and imbalances, and poor progesterone production. From an energetic medicine perspective, you should think about who or what are you holding on to that no longer benefits you? Perhaps it is a belief that no longer serves you, and your body is simply trying to wake you up to this and get you to change. So many of us fear change whether we realize it or not.

Estrogen can be a likely culprit when it comes to fluid in excess. It can also drive headaches, including migraines, increase blood clotting, decrease libido and interfere with thyroid hormone production ... big health consequences all because there is too much of one little hormone.

WHAT ROLE DOES PROGESTERONE PLAY?

Progesterone also plays a variety of roles in the human body. From a reproductive perspective, its job is to hold in place the lining of the uterus that estrogen has laid down between days one and fourteen of your cycle. If your body detects that a conception has taken place, the lining of the uterus needs to be maintained, rather than shed. As a result, progesterone levels begin to rise. If there is no conception, the lining of the uterus is not needed, and progesterone levels fall away, which initiates menstruation. When health is optimal, progesterone is the dominant sex hormone from mid-cycle onward until menstruation.

Biologically, progesterone has numerous other roles, all pivotal to the *Accidentally Overweight* message. Progesterone is a powerful antianxiety agent, an antidepressant and a diuretic, and it is essential if you are to access fat to burn it for energy. Without the right amounts you will always burn your sugar, which may break your muscles down, for energy rather than burning fat.

The relationship between sex hormones and stress hormones is fascinating and powerful, and it's where a great proportion of the physical, biochemical approach of *Accidentally Overweight* is focused. And this is because nine out of ten women who see me for consultations get very positive changes in their body and their health when we address this.

THE RELATIONSHIP BETWEEN STRESS AND SEX HORMONES

Estrogen is the dominant sex hormone between day one and day fourteen of the menstrual cycle. As described earlier, its job is to lay down the lining of the uterus and make sure there is enough body fat in the event of conception. For the first half of the menstrual cycle, a relatively small amount of progesterone is made from our adrenal glands. For the sake of this description, let's call the amount two units. Remember, the reproductive role of progesterone is to hold the lining of the uterus in place with the additional biological functions of antianxiety agent, antidepressant, diuretic, and fat burner.

However, as you now understand from the previous chapter, your adrenal glands are also where you make your stress hormones, namely adrenaline and cortisol. Adrenaline communicates to every cell of your body that your life is being threatened, even though all you may have done is shown up at work and had an unexpected deadline thrown at you, or perhaps you had an argument with your beloved and he spoke to you inappropriately because he was feeling like a failure at the time. Men usually don't behave well when they unconsciously access failure as an emotion while women typically behave in a way they (or those around them) don't like when they feel rejected. This does not excuse poor behavior, but rather offers an explanation to promote understanding.

When you are internally rattled, cortisol communicates to every cell of your body that there is no food left in the world and, as a result, it wants your body to break muscle down and store fat. Even though food is, in fact, abundant for you, and your cortisol production is likely to be coming from the areas of your life about which you feel uncertain, such as relationships, finances, or even what others might think of you, your body thinks there must be a flood, famine, or a war, as this was the only long-term stress humans historically experienced.

Since your body links progesterone to fertility, if your body's perception is that your life is under threat and that there is no food left in the world, the last thing it wants is for a woman is to conceive, so it shuts down adrenal progesterone production. Estrogen and cortisol, both signaling fat storage, remain, while you've lost the counterbalancing hormone that burns fat and gets rid of excess fluid!

I believe this situation alone is a modern day, monumental shift in female chemistry, and it can wreck havoc on a woman's emotional and physical well-being. A female goes from feeling happy, healthy, balanced, and energized, with great clarity of mind and an even mood, to having a foggy brain and feeling utterly exhausted. Physically she may feel puffy, heavy, bloated and full of fluid, with a sense that her clothes are getting tighter by the minute. And that is just the first half of the cycle!

A menstruating female ovulates around day fourteen of her cycle, and there are numerous hormonal changes that occur to drive ovulation. Once the egg has been released from the ovary, a crater remains on the surface of the ovary where the egg popped out. This crater is called the corpus luteum, and it's where the bulk of a woman's progesterone is made. Progesterone is designed to peak on day twenty-one of a twenty-eight day cycle at around twenty-five to forty units. If conception takes place, then progesterone levels need to climb to continue to hold the lining of the uterus in place. Once the placenta has formed by week 12 of gestation, progesterone levels climb to around 300 to 400 units. Pregnancy is the time when a woman has the highest level of circulating progesterone. Once a woman has birthed the placenta, however, her progesterone level plunges from 350 to zero! It is fortunate that birth brings on some other feel good hormones, although they tend to be more short-lived.

Historically, babies were welcomed into extended families and communities. Today, a more common scenario (not the only scenario) is a hospital birth followed by a new mother at home alone with her newborn during the day while her partner must continue to work to pay the bills. If there are challenges in their relationship or challenges caused by the demands of other children, financial stress, an ill newborn or simply one who won't sleep, the new home environment with baby can be highly stressful. Another stressful scenario I've heard described thousands of times is one where a new mom has made what she thought would be a welcomed transition (temporarily or permanently) from a corporate career to staying at home with her baby, but is now second-guessing her decision. The guilt and confusion around this scenario can be overwhelming. Such scenarios do not promote the restoration of adrenal progesterone levels, as the body is so busy making stress hormones that it is not "safe" for the new mom to make the fertility-linked progesterone. Remember, progesterone is one of the most powerful antianxiety and antidepressant substances the body makes. On the other hand, if Mom and baby do have support, and the new mom doesn't feel she is alone with her new precious bundle, whether this is simply due to the mother's beliefs, attitudes, and perceptions, or her actual physical support from other people, then adrenal progesterone levels are far more likely to be restored, and her chemistry is all the better for it.

If, on the other hand, conception does not take place during a menstrual cycle, then maintaining the lining of the uterus is no longer necessary, and progesterone levels fall, allowing a female to bleed. However, something that is so common today is what is known as "luteal phase insufficiency," where ovarian progesterone production is poor and a peak of 25 units in the second half of the cycle is not reached. Progesterone may be the dominant hormone from day 16 to day 18 of the cycle, but it falls away too soon (it is supposed to be dominant from around day 14 until around day 27), and estrogen becomes dominant leading into the menstrual bleed.

This estrogen dominance is the biochemical basis of pre-menstrual syndrome which causes grief for the woman as well as most people around her! When PMS occurs it can be because estrogen is dominant for all but two or three days of a twenty-eight day cycle, meaning that progesterone gets no time to rule the roost, and a woman misses out on all its delicious stress-busting and fat-burning qualities.

WHAT HAPPENS WHEN ESTROGEN IS DOMINANT?

The typical symptoms of low progesterone include:

- Premenstrual migraine
- PMS-like symptoms
- Irregular or excessively heavy periods

- Anxiety and nervousness
- A feeling like you can't get your breath past your heart

The typical symptoms of estrogen dominance (which usually also involves low progesterone—but not always) include:

- Irregular periods or excessive vaginal bleeding
- Bloating/fluid retention
- Breast swelling and/or tenderness
- Decreased libido
- Mood swings, most often irritability and depression
- Weight gain, especially around the abdomen and hips
- Cold hands and feet
- Headaches, particularly pre-menstrually
- Tendency to yellow-tinged skin

This is the most common hormonal imbalance I see in menstruating women. This shift to an estrogen-dominant cycle is also single-handedly also changing the age of onset of menstruation for young girls across the Western world. In the United States, a growing percentage of girls are starting to menstruate as young as eight years of age which is of enormous concern. The scope of this book, however, can't seek to "solve" this challenge but, for now, I merely want to highlight this "estrogen crisis" we currently face. The enormous excess of estrogen being made within the female body at earlier and earlier ages, combined with increased estrogen in our environment, appear to be affecting our endocrine (hormonal) systems in literally life-changing ways.

It is essential to discern whether a woman is suffering from symptoms of estrogen dominance caused by excess estrogen or by significantly low progesterone levels. For the latter it would mean that adrenal and/or ovarian production of progesterone is poor. This person may have optimal estrogen levels, yet they are challenged with their periods and/or their body fat due to low progesterone levels.

Another extremely common scenario is one of estrogen excess. This can come about through excessive environmental exposures, including use of the oral contraceptive pill, hormone replacement therapy, plastics, and pesticides. Another significant basis for estrogen excess is estrogen recycling as a result of poor estrogen detoxification by the liver. I will explore this in detail later; however, in a nutshell, the liver decides whether to excrete or recycle estrogen.

The liver prioritizes what it needs to detoxify, and because the body makes estrogen itself, it is not a high priority to clear it from the body. A woman can have this month's estrogen circulating as well as last month's and even from numerous previous months. Even the best progesterone producer cannot balance and keep up with so much estrogen.

An additional estrogen-dominant hormonal picture is a combination of both the descriptions above of poor progesterone production and recycled estrogen. If we took better care of our liver, this would be far less common in the Western world. As I love to say, these things have become common, but they are not normal. Women are not supposed to get PMS.

The following is an article I wrote for breast cancer awareness month. The brief I was given was to write about what makes breasts healthy. Some of it repeats information I have included earlier, but I left it here to remind you how important these factors are.

Healthy Breasts

When it comes to breast health, there is so much we now understand that contributes to the creation and maintenance of healthy breast tissue. Empowering women to take charge of this incredibly important aspect of their health is vital to the future of all women, and education must begin at a young age. Part of the challenge is deciphering fact from fiction or fad, so let's explore what we know creates healthy breasts.

Hormones, Stress, and the Liver

Although the hormone estrogen does some wonderful things for our health, too much of it or too much of a particular type of estrogen has been linked to some breast cancers. What is important to explore, when it comes to our hormones, is, why is estrogen so much more of a problem now as opposed to a time in the not so distant past? Part of the explanation lies in the production of stress hormones, and part of the explanation lies with the excretion of estrogen following liver detoxification of this substance.

When we are stressed, we make either, or both, of our two dominant stress hormones, namely adrenaline or cortisol. Adrenaline communicates to every cell of your body that your life is in danger, and cortisol tells your body that food is scarce. As a result, levels of another sex hormone called progesterone, which has been shown to be protective against breast cancer (except those that are progesterone receptor positive), falls through the floor as the body links progesterone to fertility. If the body believes that your life is in danger and that there is no more food left in the world, the last thing it wants for you is a pregnancy. And so begins part of the problem with estrogen; it is dominant in comparison to progesterone. This situation may also arise from synthetic forms of estrogen, such as from the oral contraceptive pill (OCP) or hormone replacement therapy (HRT).

The second scenario to consider involves the excretion pathway of estrogen out of the body. Once a molecule of estrogen has done its job for a specific time, it is transported to the liver where it has to be transformed so that it can be excreted. There are two phases to this detoxification process. Over the years, the workload of the liver in its second stage of this cleaning process can get clogged, just like traffic on a motorway. Where once substances flew through the liver at 70 miles per hour, they now crawl through at 15 miles per hour. When this process becomes terribly overloaded from years of too much alcohol, caffeine, refined sugar, trans fats, or the by-products of bowel congestion (a tendency to constipation), the estrogen will undergo its first stage of change, but there is no room on the second stage highway so the estrogen is released by the liver back into the blood stream. Your body is then faced with the new estrogen it continues to make from your ovaries (if you are still menstruating) and your fat cells, as well as the recycled form. It is this recycled form of estrogen that has been found to be up to

400 times higher in women with estrogen sensitive breast cancer.

Looking after your precious liver is one of the best steps you can take to ensure your breast tissue remains healthy. Sadly, many women regularly overconsume alcohol, and it is this regular, overconsumption that is undeniably linked to the development of cystic breast tissue and breast cancer. We have to get real about how much we are drinking. Heart organizations around the world suggest that two standard drinks per day (equivalent of two 100 milliliter (100 mL is the equivalent of 3.4 fl oz) glasses of wine) with two days off each week is acceptable. Cancer research suggests, however, that if you have a family history of breast cancer, there is no safe level of alcohol consumption. That is a massive statement. If alcohol is something you enjoy, don't drink it daily. Save it for special occasions. Sparkling water with fresh lemon or lime can be a great alternative.

Caffeine—coffee in particular—has also been found to play a role in the creation of denser, cystic breast tissue. On the other hand, green tea has consistently been shown in numerous studies to be protective against many types of cancers, breast cancer included. Most people are astounded at the changes in their breasts when they take a break from coffee and alcohol. As a woman living in the same world as all of you, a world with plenty of alcohol and caffeine on offer, I challenge you to take a break from these substances no matter how much you love or depend on them. Do it for one week, one little week out of your big long life. If you find that easy, do it for two. Or better still, omit them for one or two menstrual cycles and notice how different your breasts feel.

Diet and exercise

When it comes to the aspects of our diets that are essential for healthy breast tissue, vegetables and fruits head the list. All of the cruciferous vegetables (Brassica family) have potent anticancer properties. Broccoli, in particular, contains sulphoraphane, a compound that helps the body begin to eliminate carcinogenic substances from the body in as little as ten days after it is included in the diet on a daily basis. It also keeps estrogen from binding to and stimulating the growth of breast cancer cells, a vital step in keeping breast tissue healthy. The great news, too, is that sulphoraphane survives cooking. Eat broccoli people!

Eat fruits and vegetables that are also rich in beta-carotene. On average, women with breast cancer tend to have lower levels of beta-carotene in their blood, although researchers cannot say whether this is a cause or a result of the disease. A small-scale study in Italy found that beta-carotene given with other, related carotene compounds increased the tumor-free period among women who had already had breast cancer. The safest and most effective way of maintaining healthy levels of beta-carotene is to consume five or more servings of dark-green, yellow, or orange vegetables and citrus fruits daily. We must eat our vegetables every day. No excuses!

Make an effort to minimize your consumption of fried foods and charcoal-grilled meats. Also, there is evidence to suggest that reducing our consumption of animal foods and basing our diet mostly on plant-based foods is incredibly beneficial to breast health and the prevention of breast cancer.

There is a growing body of literature to suggest that insulin resistance is now a contributing factor in numerous cancers. Insulin is a hormone that can behave like a growth factor. It encourages all cells to grow: fat cells, healthy normal cells, and cells that may be precancerous or cancerous. The best way to limit insulin production in the body is to never base a meal purely on carbohydrates. The only carbs humans traditionally ate were those from berries, legumes, and pulses (we might call these lentils and beans, such as garbanzo beans). Today, we are faced with a barrage of highly processed foods, rich in sugars and starches. Limit your intake of these. We also tend to forget that most alcoholic drinks are packed with sugar.

Remember it is what you do every day that will have the most impact on your health, not what you do sometimes. It is not about going without; it is about getting real about what you, as a woman, already know to be true. You know better than anyone when you have too much of a particular substance in your diet... whether it is alcohol, coffee, or sugar. Make the changes you know you need to make now. You will give your breasts a great chance of remaining healthy in the process.

Lastly, move your body. The benefits of regular movement are well documented for many areas of our health, including a reduction in insulin levels and body fat, both of which, in excess, have been linked to unhealthy breast tissue.

Nutrients for healthy breasts

Most of us have heard about the importance of iodine for optimal thyroid function and in the prevention of goiter. What we hear very little about is how vital iodine is to breast health. The breasts concentrate iodine as do the ovaries, and studies have shown that a form of estrogen associated with breast cancer can be produced by the ovaries in an iodine-deficient state. This has been shown to be reversible once iodine levels are optimal again. Use a salt that contains iodine, add seaweeds to cooking, or take a supplement.

Also of great consequence to breast health is our dietary intake and ratio of essential fatty acids. These are predominantly found in oily fish, flaxseeds, walnuts and pecans, evening primrose oil, and borage oil. It can be difficult to eat enough of these vital fats on a daily basis, so a good supplement combining at least fish or flax with evening primrose oils can be a great addition to your daily diet. Start with two capsules in the morning and two at night.

Another mineral that is essential for healthy breast tissue is magnesium and, coupled with selenium, these nutrients have been shown to reduce the incidences of new breast cancers. Green, leafy vegetables are high in magnesium, while brazil nuts are rich in selenium. Eat them daily, or take a supplement.

Vitamin C is one of the most important nutrients when it comes to so many aspects of our health. The list of wonderful activities vitamin C performs in the body is almost endless. It helps keep the immune system responding appropriately to stimuli, and hastens white blood cell response times.

Vitamin B6 has also been extensively researched when it comes to breast health. Eggs are a good source, as are bananas and avocados.

Herbs for healthy breasts

Two of my most favorite herbs work on the adrenal glands. These are rhodiola and the Ginseng family. Both herbs are considered to be adaptogens, which means they help the body adapt to stressors by fine-tuning the stress response. These herbs tend to have a calming effect on the central nervous system, which in turn promotes appropriate sex and stress hormone production rather than extremes.

Other herbs that have been shown to be useful in creating healthy breast tissue are those that promote liver detoxification and bile production from the gall bladder. Bile is essential for the appropriate excretion of any fat-soluble substances from the body, including cholesterol and estrogen. Useful herbs include St Mary's thistle, Globe artichoke, Bupleurum and Schisandra.

Minimize exposure to...

The final thing you need to know about the creation and maintenance of healthy breast tissue involves the things that are best kept to a minimum wherever possible. Minimizing our exposure to growth factor-like substances, including insulin, may be an important aspect of maintaining healthy breast tissue. Dairy products naturally contain growth factors, since the milk is designed to grow a 90 pound baby calf into a nearly 2000 pound beast.

The growth factors naturally present in milk and milk products drive this growth. Humans, however, aren't designed to grow at these rates. If milk must be consumed, sheep and goats are smaller animals so their milks tend to drive slower, smaller growth rates. Alternatively, nut milks contain no growth factors. For people with diabetes who need insulin, eating a diet that limits the need for insulin without, however, compromising blood glucose levels is important.

There is also a growing and very concerning body of evidence that points at the importance of minimizing our exposure to plastics and pesticides. They disrupt our endocrine (hormonal) systems and can mimic estrogen. Recent research out of the United States shows that a large percentage of girls aged eight have hit puberty, leading to longer estrogen production over their lifetime. Furthermore, fewer pregnancies also lead to relatively more time spent in estrogen-dominant states. Researchers suggest that poor diet, lack of exercise, high body fat, and exposure to plastics are the likely culprits for the earlier onset of menstruation. We can make a really big difference to our health and our children's health by getting these lifestyle factors on track.

There are numerous reproductive conditions that involve poor progesterone production or estrogen dominance in some way. Polycystic ovarian syndrome (PCOS) and endometriosis are two frequently diagnosed, but quite different, conditions.

Polycystic ovarian syndrome

In PCOS, the eggs in the ovaries ripen on the surface of the ovary but are not released. They harden and form cysts (hence the name of the condition). As you now understand, to obtain optimal progesterone levels, ovulation is essential, since the majority of your monthly progesterone is made by the corpus luteum.

Other hormones are also involved in PCOS. The pituitary gland, which sits at the base of the brain, makes luteinizing hormone (LH) and follicle stimulating hormone (FSH). Just prior to day fourteen of a typical cycle, both hormones increase, but in PCOS both these hormones from the pituitary gland tend to flatline. Testosterone, the dominant male sex hormone, also tends to be slightly higher in women with PCOS.

The LH and FSH hormonal profile of an ideal menstrual cycle is illustrated in the figure below while the profile of someone with PCOS is represented in the second figure.

Normal Menstrual Cycle

Ideal LH and FSH peaks generating ovulation:
Both LH and FSH peak to drive ovulation.

PCOS

A Typical PCOS LH and FSH Profile:
*Both LH and FSH tend to flatline in PCOS with LH levels
remaining consistently elevated.*

When it comes to challenges with the reproductive system or hormones, I find exploring unconscious beliefs and examining behaviors for each individual very useful. This is nowhere clearer than in PCOS. I often explain to my clients that there is nothing more feminine than our ovaries; men don't have them. With PCOS, however, it is as if the ovaries have gone deaf. The pituitary gland stops trying to alert the ovaries to release an egg, the most feminine process that goes on inside a woman. For the ovaries to no longer hear the call from the pituitary, there could be a very silent, unconscious belief from somewhere in this person's world that they have to behave like a man in order to receive appreciation, connection, or love. Somewhere in their past, more masculine behavior has been rewarded. Women are incredibly capable. They have shown they can match it with men in every arena. But there are types of work that, even today, are still more male dominated. I have met countless women, working in these male-dominated industries in particular, whose hormonal profile has taken on a decidedly masculine appearance. These women, as I said are incredibly capable. The problem, however, lies in their (usually unconscious) beliefs about how they have to be in order to perform and achieve. Most often, they do not even realize that they are thinking or behaving "like a man" until we explore what that looks like.

Our chemistry is ancient. What we ask of our body today is entirely different from what we asked of it even fifty years ago. On the one hand, it is truly remarkable what our body can do: work sixteen-hour days sitting at a desk, constantly think up solutions to challenges presented during the day, meet deadlines, juggle phone calls, crises, and complaints, and hopefully also celebrate a few things. And this is just the tip of the iceberg. On the other hand, we are so very far removed from the way humans have lived for 149,950 years that I believe the human body is rebelling, and one of the most obvious areas is women's reproductive health.

If this rings true for you, explore ways you can bring more feminine rituals into your life. What do you associate with femininity? If you need to be "masculine" at work, do it. Try instead to simply soften your mind when you're there. No one will know this is what you've done. Don't look at the work on your desk and tense up. Instead, notice the work on your desk and take a long slow breath that moves your belly when you inhale. Relax into it. Only you know you've done this. Your productivity and contribution will still be enormous and perhaps even more than what you found possible from a state of tension. Think about "creating" instead of "producing." In emotional medicine, the ovaries are the seats of creativity. Just that shift in language is more feminine.

When you come home, be a complete girl! Light a candle and notice the fragrance. Dance around your house to music you love! Have a bubble bath. Giggle with the children or at a comedy. Read a girly book if that appeals to you. Make a pot of herbal tea after dinner in a teapot you love, and turn it into an "occasion." Notice the design of the pot and cup, the fragrance, and how you feel taking care of yourself. Masculinity (not men, but masculine energy) would never do this. But a man embracing his feminine would, just to point out the difference.

Please understand, this not an anti-feminist concept. Addressing the biochemistry of PCOS is of enormous importance to getting health results. I simply wanted to highlight the incredible benefit I have witnessed when women embrace their feminine essence in more areas of their lives. And feminine rituals are a beautiful place to start. I encourage all women with PCOS to explore what they perceive their fathers expected of them or whom they had to be to "earn" his love. And then breathe, soften, and relax.

ENDOMETRIOSIS

Endometriosis is a condition where the tissue that is destined to line the uterus grows in areas outside the uterus. Just as the tissue that is laid down to line the uterus each month receives hormonal signals about when to shed, any uterine tissue that has been laid down elsewhere, such as around the fallopian tubes or attached to the bowel, also receives the same hormonal signals and this tissue also bleeds, which can be an intensely painful process. Furthermore, each area of tissue behaves like a little estrogen factory, adding to the already established estrogen-dominant hormonal picture.

PUBERTY

Some girls breeze through this time of transition without much change in their moods or their bodies, while, for others, an anxiety or even a darkness can set in. Estrogen is the first female sex hormone to be made in any great quantity in a girl's body. As beautiful as estrogen can be as a hormone, it can wreck havoc when it is present in substantial amounts for the first time ever, in young female bodies that do not yet have sufficient progesterone being made to counterbalance its effects.

Prior to menstruation beginning, estrogen is being

made causing the breasts to bud and promoting the growth of pubic hair. It also begins to drive fat storage for all of the reasons outlined earlier. Some girls appear to be more "fleshy" for a time just prior to menarche, indicating estrogen is fulfilling its role.

Because progesterone is a powerful antianxiety agent and an antidepressant, if it is slow to initiate, a girl who was once bouncy, bright, full of energy, and interested in things, can become flat in her moods and distant in her relationships. If her periods do begin and they are irregular and/or heavy and painful, to the extent she is unable cope with school or life in general, she will often be encouraged to go on the oral contraceptive pill. It is important to understand two things here. One is the way the contraceptive pills work and the second is the biochemical process that occurs at the onset of menstruation.

Firstly, the pill is successful at preventing pregnancy because it shuts down the ovarian production of hormones. The number of women of all ages I meet who have no idea how this powerful medication works astounds me. I am neither pro-pill nor anti-pill; I simply want people to make informed choices. I will say it again. The pill shuts down ovarian production of hormones, and the body relies entirely on the synthetic version of hormones being supplied by the tablet. Substances in patented medications, such as the pill, must be at least ten percent different from the form the body naturally makes. They are not identical to the way the body makes it.

With the ovaries shut down, the adrenal production of progesterone becomes even more important yet is unlikely to be optimal given what can be a stressful time around the onset of menstruation and, for some girls, the increase in body fat for the first time. Never never *ever* comment on an adolescent girl's changing shape and size by encouraging her to eat less. That stresses her more as she may feel like she is letting you down when she doesn't do it; it doesn't matter whether you are her parent, teacher, or friend. Explain that, for a while, hormones can change our shapes, and eating nutritious food and staying active are the most important things to do to stay healthy. With less stress, which may be caused by her private perception of how her life is, which may gently be explored, her progesterone is more likely to kick in, and her body shape and size will sort itself out. Some areas that can be useful to explore in this situation is an adolescent female's perception of academic pressure and her perception of what it may mean to a family member if she "fails" (which may mean not coming out on top of her class in some cases). Exploring what her "friends" are saying at school can also prove insightful.

The second issue that needs to be explored is the biochemistry associated with the onset of menstruation. This is the first time in a girl's life that her pituitary gland sends signals to her ovaries. For approximately the first five years, the chemical messengers released by the pituitary follow a road to the ovaries that looks like a goat track, meaning that it is a path that sometimes reaches a destination (in this case the ovaries) and sometimes winds up heading off into no man's land. In other words, sometimes the pituitary signals miss their mark. After about five years, this pathway, if it has been allowed to become established, behaves like a five-lane highway. The route is clear, straight, and unhindered.

What I see, though, time and time again, are girls who have gone onto the pill to manage irregular or very heavy periods rather than for contraception, shortly after menstruation begins. If sport is a big issue or school is being missed due to severe period pain, then perhaps there may be occasions when the use of the pill is appropriate, and I certainly do not want to illicit feelings of guilt in parents or daughters in this area! But! The pill simply masks the truth. If a girl stays on the pill long-term, the five-lane highway is never established. She will then come off the pill in adulthood wanting to have babies, but her pituitary has no history of communicating with her ovaries. It is a lot to ask our ovaries to suddenly wake up when we have suppressed their function for an extended period of time.

I cannot encourage you enough to get to the bottom of *why* the pain or the irregularity occurs in the first place. Before deciding about whether or not the pill is the best choice, explore other options and seek ways to change the hormonal imbalance that may be present, or at least give the pituitary-ovary pathway time to get established.

As far as moods are concerned, what breaks my heart is seeing a young woman start menstruating, with very heavy periods and some weight gain despite still eating well, disappear into her mind with her own private focus on sad thoughts. This can be the first time ever that a girl experiences a tendency to depression, and her family is often bereft and concerned at the change in their girl. The most common intervention in this situation is the prescription of the pill. But because the pill does not correct what is likely to be slow-starting or insufficient progesterone, the young woman's mood doesn't lift, despite her periods now being regulated (by the pill). So she is encouraged by well-meaning adults to take an antidepressant. She is not even halfway through her teens, and she is on two incredibly potent medications.

There are times when conventional medicine is lifesaving, and I am not suggesting it be avoided at all costs, especially not at the cost of precious human life. What I am encouraging, initially, is the balancing of estrogen and progesterone through natural methods with an experienced health professional. Counseling at the same time may also be incredibly beneficial to assist with the new darker thoughts that may have arisen. My holistic approach means also discussing any fears this young woman may have about her perception of what it means to be an adult woman. It can also be the first time she ever feels fleshy, puffy, or bloated, and, to a young mind influenced so heavily by popular magazines, it is easy to understand why she can think she is fat when all she is, is estrogen dominant. As I said earlier, it is not physically possible to gain six pounds of fat in one day. It is most likely due to fluid and, given the diuretic action of progesterone, a deficiency of this vital hormone is one of the likely culprits of this young woman's fleshy feelings.

MENOPAUSE

At its simplest level, menopause is the ceasing of the ovarian production of hormones. But production continues from the adrenal glands. However, as explained earlier, many women now make insufficient amounts of progesterone in their adrenals because of chronic stress. In my opinion, this is such a powerful factor in whether a woman breezes through menopause with few or no debilitating symptoms, or whether the heat and the sleeplessness become overwhelming. If you are approaching menopause, I cannot encourage you enough to ensure your adrenal function is optimal. Apply the adrenal care techniques described earlier in this book, using breathing strategies and herbal support, combined with lifestyle changes where possible.

If you are post-menopausal, I also can't encourage you enough to address adrenal health and liver health (covered in the next chapter). Heat from the body can certainly be due to low estrogen levels or liver congestion. If I meet a client who has tried all sorts of natural estrogen therapies and used herbs that have an estrogenic action such as Black cohosh, and they are still overwhelmingly hot and suffering debilitating hot flashes, I will treat their liver with the strategies outlined in the chapter on the liver.

Remember that in traditional circles, menopause is a time when wisdom begins to flow constantly. Trust what you already know inside of you when it comes to your health. You innately know better than anyone else what is best for you. Seek guidance from health professionals, but apply only what makes sense to you.

Menstruation and menopause are feminine and very natural processes. They offer an incredible insight into a woman's general health as well as a window into her inner world of unconscious thoughts and beliefs. These thoughts and beliefs drive so much of what we do and how we feel. They can be a barometer guiding her to remember what she was born knowing ... that she is loveliness embodied.

SOLUTIONS FOR SEX HORMONES

- If you have any type of menstrual cycle or reproductive system challenges, take a four-week break from alcohol or, better still, take a break from it for two menstrual cycles. You'll see your PMS significantly decrease.

- If this solution is "impossible," decrease alcohol intake to two nights a week, and preferably drink less than half a bottle of wine. I meet so many women who drink a minimum of half a bottle of wine every night. We were never designed to drink in this way. Decrease it.

- Coffee can be another big-ticket item when it comes to PMS, via liver congestion. Consider swapping coffee for green tea for four weeks, and see how you feel.

For estrogen dominance (which can be confirmed with a saliva or a blood test):
- Diindolylmethane (DIM), an extract of broccoli.

I am all for getting what we need from our food, but, in this case, you need to eat eight heads of broccoli a day to get the same therapeutic effect as one good quality capsule of DIM. Lance Armstrong is the only person I've heard of who has done that! In fact, he attributes part of his extraordinary recovery from cancer to how much broccoli he ate! Get into it, people!

- For PMS, the following table is useful. You may experience one or a number of different PMS patterns at once.

MENOPAUSE STRATEGIES

- For hot flashes consider whether the heat is coming from low estrogen, liver/gall bladder congestion, or both?

    o For low estrogen, Black Cohosh and Sage can be useful.

    o For the liver/gall bladder, Globe Artichoke, St Mary's thistle, Bupleurum, and Schisandra are excellent.

- For adrenal support, Rhodiola can be brilliant if you are also exhausted or Siberian ginseng or Withania

- For low blood pressure, Licorice is excellent

- Magnesium

For all the challenges discussed in this chapter, focus on the gifts of your feminine essence.

The different types of PMS:
the mechanisms involved, and the potential treatments

	Symptoms	Mechanism	Potential Treatment
PMS-1	Anxiety Nervous tension Irritability Mood swings Insomnia	Elevated estrogen Low progesterone High cortisol	Vitex Dong quai Vitamin B DIM
PMS-2	Water and sodium retention Abdominal bloating Weight gain Breast tenderness	Elevated aldosterone (fluid) Low dopamine	Dandelion leaves Vitamin B Vitex Rhodiola
PMS-3	Craving for sweets Increased appetite Can't resist refined sugar, followed by palpitation and fatigue Dizziness, shakiness, headache	Low magnesium Deficiency of prostaglandin PGE1 (low in an anti-inflammatory substance) Elevated insulin	Magnesium Essential fats; UDO's oil or fish oil or a flax oil and evening primrose oil combination Cinnamon
PMS-4	Period pain and clots	Elevated prostaglandin PGE2 (pro-inflammatory; increases inflammation in the body) Deficiency of anti-inflammatory substances Possible magnesium deficiency	Bupleurum if clots Dong quai Magnesium Essential fats, fish oil, flax oil if vegetarian

The Liver
Puzzle piece 4

W hen it comes to fat burning, the liver packs a mighty punch. In conjunction with the gall bladder, it works endlessly to help us excrete fatty substances, including stored body fat. The best way to imagine the fat-burning power of the liver somewhat accurately is to picture a triangle shape on its side and inside that triangle are billions and billions of little circles, each one of them a liver cell. Inside each liver cell is a mouse on a wheel running and running and running, and each turn of the billions of little wheels is driving your metabolism.

When we treat our liver unkindly, a circle can die. For a time, the liver can regenerate a dead cell, but, after a while, this is no longer possible, and a globule of fat will take up residence where once that fat-burning little "mouse" was working. When many fat globules take over the liver (known as "fatty liver"), our body fat deposition pattern shifts. For the first time, people notice that they have a fat roll quite high up on their abdomen. For women, this is just below their bra and, for men, just beneath their pectoral muscles. It can come and go, and sometimes there is a point right in the centre of your torso that is tender. I will always suggest ways to support your liver based on the presence of a fat roll in that position and gall bladder support based on that tender point. It is not, however, only fat burning itself where the liver plays a role in body fat management. The liver also guides other areas of metabolism, including cholesterol and estrogen, which are important to understand when it comes to accessing fat to burn.

THE NUTRIENTS YOU NEED FOR DETOXIFICATION

The liver is the body's second largest organ after our skin and it sits just behind your right rib cage. Its primary role is detoxification, a concept surrounded by much confusion. Detoxification is a process that goes on inside us, all day every day, and is essentially a transformation process. Any substance that would be harmful to you if it were to accumulate in your body is changed by the liver into a less harmful form so it can then be excreted safely from your body and removed forever. The choices we make influence how efficiently the liver is able to do its job.

There are two stages to the detoxification process, appropriately named Phase 1 and Phase 2 liver detoxification processes. Both stages require certain nutrients to function, and dietary choices can influence how efficiently each phase is able to proceed. The figure below illustrates the phases of detoxification.

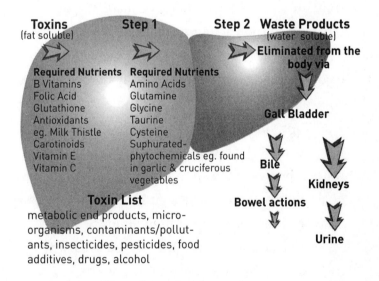

Toxins (fat soluble) **Step 1** **Step 2** **Waste Products** (water soluble)
Eliminated from the body via

Required Nutrients
B Vitamins
Folic Acid
Glutathione
Antioxidants
eg. Milk Thistle
Carotinoids
Vitamin E
Vitamin C

Required Nutrients
Amino Acids
Glutamine
Glycine
Taurine
Cysteine
Suphurated-
phytochemicals eg. found
in garlic & cruciferous
vegetables

Gall Bladder

Bile

Kidneys

Toxin List
metabolic end products, micro-
organisms, contaminants/pollut-
ants, insecticides, pesticides, food
additives, drugs, alcohol

Bowel actions

Urine

Liver detoxification pathways:
Phase 1 and Phase 2 liver detoxification pathways and the nutrients essential to these vital processes.

For the first stage of detoxification, numerous nutrients, including B vitamins, are essential. Grains are one of the richest sources of B vitamins we have in the food supply, yet many people feel much better with fewer of these foods in their diets. People decrease or cut grains out of their diets for varied reasons. Some first experienced rapid weight loss with the advent of the high protein, very low carbohydrate diets, purported as the answer to all of our weight loss desires in the late 1990s, a repeat of the popular dietary concept from the 1970s. Some people simply started to notice that foods made from grains gave them reflux or made their tummy bloated and took action to change how they felt.

If grains feel good for you and energize you, then enjoy them in whole food form. If they don't suit you, don't eat them. Your body knows best what works for you. Simply be aware that if you have a low intake of B vitamins, your Phase 1 liver detoxification processes may not function optimally. It can be useful to take a supplement if you eat a low carbohydrate diet or avoid or limit grains.

There is one road into the liver and five pathways out of it. Just as for Phase 1 reactions, Phase 2 liver pathways also require certain nutrients to function, in particular, specific amino acids and sulfur.

Really think about this next statement. *What*

we eat becomes part of us. The protein foods you eat are broken down into amino acids, and one of the things they go on to create is all of the cells of your immune system, which is what defends you from infection. Amino acids also go on to create the neurotransmitters in your brain that influence your mood and clarity of thought. They also build your muscles so that you can carry anything and everything. It really does matter what we eat. Your food becomes part of you.

The sulfur you need for Phase 2 liver detoxification can be obtained from eggs, onions, garlic, and shallots, as well as the *brassica* family of vegetables, which includes broccoli, cabbage, kale, brussels sprouts, and cauliflower. The liver makes enzymes that are responsible for the transformation of each substance, and the rate of production of these essential enzymes determines how quickly each substance is processed. The load placed on the liver also determines how quickly things move through the liver.

LIVER LOADERS

There is a group of substances I lovingly label as "liver loaders." Can you guess what they are? They include:

- Alcohol
- Caffeine

- Trans fats

- Sugars, including fructose and sucrose (see the insulin chapter for further explanation)

- Synthetic substances, such as pesticides, medications, skin "care"

- Infection, for example viruses such as glandular fever (Epstein-Barr virus, Mononucleosis)

When it comes to pesticides we are guinea pigs with regards to the long-term consumption of these substances. The reason your apple looks so perfect is because it has been sprayed to make it that way. We cannot see or taste the chemicals on its skin, but they are there. Pesticides have to be tested before they can be used on food for human consumption. However, they are often tested for such a short amount of time that I do not believe we can compare tests done over, say, a six-month period, to being exposed to these things over our entire lifetime. What also cannot be tested is what happens when all of the chemicals are mixed and they are mixed inside our bodies every day when we eat conventionally grown produce. Fresh food the way it comes in nature is an incredibly important part of our diets, and I simply want to encourage people to choose organic produce whenever they can. Also, think about the way you eat the food. We peel a banana. It may have been sprayed, but how much gets through the skin? We actually don't know. But surely there would be less chemical residue in the flesh (inside) of a banana than on the skin. So perhaps choosing a conventionally grown banana is not too bad. Yet when it comes to an apple, we usually eat the whole fruit. So you would be better to choose an organic (or biodynamically grown) apple wherever possible.

Think about this. Organic food is the true cost of food. I once started and ran an organic café. Once a week, a local farmer delivered fresh greens picked that morning from his biodynamic farm. I always set aside some time on the day of his delivery to chat with him, as he always had wonderful tales to tell of life on his farm. One day, when I asked him how he was, his reply was along the lines of "not so good." When I enquired further, he went on to tell me that snails had invaded his broccoli patch virtually overnight. When I paused to consider this, I realized that, if they took hold, a portion of this man's meager livelihood would be lost. So I asked him how he deals with snails on his broccoli given that his farming principles do not involve spraying the patch to get rid of the invaders (which would have taken less than thirty minutes to do). My farmer friend went on to tell me that snails lose their "stick," their ability to suction on to things, in salty water. So he made up a bottle of salt and water, and he spent two days, crouched down on all fours, crawling between his broccoli plants, squirting saline water up under the fronds. Not only that, he didn't kill the snails but collected them in a bucket and fed them to the chickens "to keep them in the food chain" as he so delightfully put it. Think about each of these scenarios. Spray in under thirty minutes versus crawling around on your haunches for two days. For me, that illustrates precisely why organic and biodynamic food costs more. It reflects the real cost of food, plus it has a greater nutritional value. The more of us who choose it, the cheaper it will become. The more we demand organic and say no to chemicals, the more organics will have to be supplied. I know I'm on my soapbox, and I really do want to remain real and practical with the advice I offer. So, in simple terms, choose organic food whenever you can.

If organic food is unavailable in your area or it is too costly for you to buy, try this solution to remove pesticides. Pesticides tend to be fat-soluble and general washing, which can get rid of dirt and germs, does not remove them. To clean food of both dirt and pesticides at the same time, fill your sink with three parts water to one part vinegar, and wash your fruits and vegetables. Then rinse them in fresh water, pat them dry, and store them for use. Do what is practical for you.

Another consideration in the liver-loading department of synthetic substances, are the substances we use for skin care. We're crazy if we think that we don't absorb things through our skin. You only have to look at the way nicotine patches work to realize that the skin is a quick and easy route to our blood stream, carrying the blood that the liver will need to clean. There are plenty of wonderful skin care companies out there that do not use synthetic ingredients. Seek them out. I love to suggest to people that it would be good if they could eat their skin care!

It is not, however, just the things we consume or the things we put on our skin that can place demands on the detoxification processes of the liver. Substances your body makes itself also need transformation by the liver so they can be excreted. These substances include:

- Cholesterol
- Steroid hormones such as estrogen
- Any shortfall in digestion/bowel congestion/ irritable bowel syndrome (IBS)

I have met countless people who have not consumed much in the way of consumed liver loaders, but they still have diabolical menstrual cycles or an ongoing challenge with IBS or constipation, and exhibit what I consider to be very distinct signs that their liver needs support. Passing clots while menstruating is a classic liver congestion sign. These are listed at the conclusion of this chapter. My point is, if your body tries to protect your liver by producing excess cholesterol or if your bowels have been the bane of your life for many years, it is likely that you would feel much better and your clothes would become looser if some liver support strategies we employed.

CHOLESTEROL

Cholesterol is an extremely important substance. We only ever hear bad press about cholesterol; however, we would melt without it. It is the building block of all of our steroid (sex) hormones, including progesterone and testosterone. The process that cholesterol undergoes to form steroid hormones is illustrated in the diagram following.

Cholesterol Metabolism:
the creation of steroid hormones from cholesterol.

The reason I included the above biochemical diagram is to literally illustrate the way substances in the body flow on to create other substances. Cholesterol that the body makes, or that you obtain from your diet, does not always remain as cholesterol. In fact, you do not want too much cholesterol accumulating as cholesterol. You want it to turn into progesterone, testosterone, DHEA, and estrogen (all of the words in the diagram that begin with "est" are different forms of estrogen).

Your diet contributes to approximately 20 percent of the amount of cholesterol in your blood, while your liver creates the other 80 percent. Your liver makes cholesterol when it needs to protect itself and, in such situations, cholesterol behaves like an anti-inflammatory. What are some of the things that may inflame the liver and drive additional cholesterol production? We listed them above! One of the most successful ways to reduce your blood level of cholesterol is to take extra good care of your liver and deal with any inflammation in the body with a good-quality essential fat supplement, outlined in the solutions section later in this chapter. There are two mechanisms involved in the accumulation of cholesterol outlined below.

Based on the cholesterol metabolism flow chart on the previous page, healthy cholesterol metabolism is best imagined as a gently flowing stream. You want a small amount of cholesterol to remain in your blood as cholesterol, but you want the majority of the cholesterol to be converted into your steroid hormones. Men and women make all three of the major sex hormones—specifically testosterone, estrogen and progesterone—they just make them in differing ratios, with men producing more testosterone and far less estrogen with some progesterone, while women make more estrogen and progesterone and less testosterone. You can see from the cholesterol diagram above that certain enzymes push the hormones one way or the other. Sometimes over time, however, cholesterol can accumulate as cholesterol. To come back to the analogy of cholesterol metabolism being like a flowing stream, it is as if a dam wall gets built across the flow and, instead of cholesterol being converted into sex hormones, it accumulates in the blood as cholesterol. There are two problems here.

One is that too much blood cholesterol may pose a health problem (although the jury is out on whether this is actually true with regard to heart disease), and the other is that you now have lower levels of sex hormones being produced. Since your steroid (sex) hormones make you feel vital and alive, they play an enormous role in whether you bounce (or stagger) out of bed each morning. When you have optimal levels of, and balanced, sex hormones, you feel amazing.

For cholesterol to be converted into sex hormones, you must have optimal zinc levels, and essential fatty acids are also important. Our best sources of the omega 3 fats are the oils in fish, flaxseeds (linseeds), walnuts, and pecans, while evening primrose oil and borage oil are good sources of the omega 6 type. The richest food source of zinc is oysters. Beef and lamb also contain some, and vegetable sources include seeds, such as sunflower seeds and pumpkin seeds. As far as amounts go, however, oysters contain (on average) seventy milligrams of zinc per 100 grams, whereas beef, the next best source of zinc, contains only four milligrams. Lamb has on average 2.9 milligrams zinc; seeds have around 0.9 milligrams of zinc per 100 grams. In the not so distant past, we obtained consistent amounts of zinc from our plants foods. But food is only as good as the quality of the soil, and if a nutrient is not in the soil, then it can't be in our food! Most soil in the Western world is deficient in zinc unless it has been organically or, better still from a zinc perspective, biodynamically farmed. Each adult needs a minimum of fifteen milligrams of zinc per day, just so the body can perform its basic functions. That is potentially not even enough for optimal health. So from where on earth are we getting our zinc? The answer is, many of us are not. Studies have suggested that approximately 70 percent of people living in Western countries are deficient in zinc, even though it is a mineral that is not only essential for keeping cholesterol levels in check and producing optimal amounts of sex hormones, but it is also vital for our skin and wound healing, as well as digestion and immune function. Zinc is a mighty little mineral!

The second part of this biochemical picture about cholesterol metabolism and liver health involves the excretion of cholesterol. The same mechanism also applies to estrogen—so for any female who read the previous chapter and identified estrogen dominance in her life, this is incredibly important.

When a liver loader, either consumed (exogenous) or endogenous (made as a result of internal chemistry) arrives at the front door of the liver, it has arrived to be changed! Alcohol, in particular, must be changed as a priority, since the human body is unable to excrete it. I do not make the following statement lightly; it is simply a fact. *Alcohol is a poison to the human body*. We cannot excrete it. To do so it must be changed into acetaldehyde. Acetaldehyde is the substance that can accumulate and cause a headache/hangover the day after excessive imbibing.

So when any of the liver loaders (in this case, let's remain focused on cholesterol) arrive at the front door of the liver, they undergo the first stage of change (Phase 1 liver detoxification). Between the front door and the middle of the liver, cholesterol is still cholesterol, although it has been slightly changed. This slightly changed cholesterol then wants to go down one of the five Phase 2 detox roads and, once it has done that, it has been slightly changed again, and it is this substance that can then be excreted and gone from your body forever.

Health problems can arise, however, when the traffic on the Phase 2 pathways get jammed like traffic on a highway. After years of routine consumption of liver loaders, hormonal or bowel problems, the roads out of the liver can become congested. Conventional blood tests for liver function do not show this. The liver takes years of battering before conventional blood tests reflect the congestion that lead to them becoming elevated in the first place. When the traffic is jammed, the cholesterol (or estrogen) undergoes its first stage of change and arrives in the middle of the liver, ready to go down its appropriate path for the second stage of the transformation it must undergo before it can be excreted. If the Phase 2 pathways are clogged, the cholesterol (or estrogen) sitting in the middle of the liver has nowhere to go, but it cannot remain waiting in the middle of the liver as there is more rubbish constantly coming through the front door. When this happens, the liver then releases the cholesterol (or estrogen) back into the blood and the recycling of cholesterol or estrogen begins. It is the recycling of these substances, not the substances themselves, that is potentially harmful to human health. What organ can we take much better care of if we want to stop this recycling from happening? Our precious liver.

On another note, it is the recycled form of estrogen that is of such concern for women regarding the risk of developing reproductive cancers. Estrogen is a beautiful hormone in the right amount and with the right types of estrogen being dominant. Too much total estrogen or too much of the wrong type are the problems, because of the estrogen itself and also because progesterone production can never match it. Our livers need more love and less of a load.

ANTI-OXIDANT DEFENSE MECHANISMS

The other way the body detoxifies (other than through Phase 1 and 2 detoxification pathways) is through our antioxidant defense mechanisms. This is a superb aspect of our chemistry. Humans stay alive through a process called respiration, meaning that we breathe in oxygen, and we exhale carbon dioxide. If you could see oxygen in space, it is two O's (two oxygen molecules) stuck together. The diagram below illustrates what I am about to describe.

$$O_2$$

$$O = O$$

$$O^- \text{ (free radical)}$$

A/O (antioxidant/donator)

$$O = O$$

$$O_2$$

Free Radical Protection from Anti-oxidants:
The oxygen donation of anti-oxidants.

When we breathe, oxygen splits apart, forming two single oxygen molecules. These are known as free radicals, and they are angry little critters, as they have lost their buddy. They have the potential to damage your tissues. One of the main ways the body defends itself from damage by a free radical is through the consumption of antioxidants. Antioxidant-rich foods are our colored plant foods. Blueberries, green tea, red wine, and chocolate are rich in antioxidants and the most common antioxidant-rich foods called out at my live events when I ask the audience for ideas! It is the skins and seeds of red grapes that are especially high in antioxidants, so grape juice is just as powerful as red wine (from an antioxidant perspective!). If you could imagine a large platter covered in beautiful, brightly colored fresh produce, that platter would pack an antioxidant punch! The way it works is that the antioxidant donates one of its oxygens back to the single guy (free radical) and they pair up. The oxygen is as happy as a duck, and will no longer damage your tissues. Isn't that magical?

To understand one powerful way free radicals can damage our tissues is to imagine a blood vessel leading to your heart. A free radical zips about through the blood and suddenly does a dive bomb and makes an indentation in the wall of the vessel. It resembles the divot in the grass beneath a golf swing that has taken too much soil with it. The damaged vessel sends out a cry for help, and, in this case, cholesterol wants to be the hero. Cholesterol behaves like a Band-aid in this situation, coming along and sticking itself over the top of the injured site. It then sends out a message to all of its cholesterol friends to join the Band-aid party, and they too come and stick themselves over the top of the first cholesterol globule that arrived. The cholesterol piles up, and then it oxidizes and hardens. This is called atherosclerosis or plaque, and it narrows the interior of the arteries. Where once the blood could flow through a wide, open vessel, it now has a very narrow, restricted path to follow. Your blood is the only way for oxygen and nutrients to get around your body. Your heart is a muscle, and it needs both oxygen and nutrients to survive. If it is starved of either of these for long enough, this is one way we can go on to have a heart attack.

The good news, though, is that this condition is reversible. The hardened, built up cholesterol is LDL cholesterol, which is why it is commonly known as "bad" cholesterol. "Good" cholesterol (HDL cholesterol) comes along and unsticks each globule of cholesterol and carries it off. Where to? You guessed it ... the liver. It arrives at the front door of the liver to undergo its detoxification process and, when the liver is functioning well, the cholesterol is processed, excreted, and gone forever. However, if the liver is loaded up with substances with higher priority up the detox order than boring old, home-made cholesterol (which is most other substances entering the liver), then the cholesterol reaches the mid-point of the liver, is released too soon, and gets reabsorbed. And that is one major way our blood cholesterol goes up and up and up. Cholesterol can also be elevated when thyroid function is poor.

The following is an article I wrote about alcohol that was published in a January issue of a magazine.

Alcohol

As the festive season draws to a close, the effects of too much alcohol may still be silently, or loudly, reverberating. Whether it is increased body fat or cellulite, less energy and vitality, worse bouts of PMS or mood fluctuations... or perhaps your get up and go has got up and left. As fun as it can be at the time, alcohol can rob you of your clarity and purpose. And so January often sees us making big statements about our health, alcohol reduction, or avoidance. Some wait until February to take a break, as they've worked out it has the least number of days! I know others who do Oct-sober in October.

We drink for wide and varied reasons.

For some, it is the way they socialize, or the way they wind down from the day. Some use alcohol to distract themselves from thoughts and feelings they'd rather avoid. It can be a way that people cope. Regardless of the reason, many of us over-drink without even realizing it.

A standard drink is one hundred grams of alcohol in whatever form that comes. In New Zealand and Australia one hundred grams of alcohol is a 330-millilitre bottle of 4 percent beer, a thirty-milliliter nip of spirits, 170 milliliters of champagne, and it is a measly 100 milliliters of wine—about four swallows! Next time you pour yourself a glass of wine, measure it, and see what your natural pour is. For most, it is considerably more than 100 milliliters, and, as a result, many of us are over-drinking without even realizing.

The current recommendations provided by Heart Foundations say that for women, no more than two standard drinks per day with two alcohol free days (AFDs) per week is okay, while for men, three standard drinks per day and two alcohol free days is acceptable.

We have long heard the heart-health benefits of red wine publicly sung, and somehow it justifies to us that drinking is okay—you are clearly looking after your heart. Also consider the American Cancer Society's position statement on alcohol. It is very powerful and they "recommend" even less is consumed.

I'm not suggesting you don't drink alcohol. Alcohol consumption can be immensely pleasurable for those who partake. I simply want to appeal to you to get honest with yourself about how alcohol affects you. You know in your heart if you drink too much and when it is impacting negatively on your health. Alcohol can affect the way we relate to those we love the most in the world, and of course it affects how you feel about yourself. So, if you drink, drink for the pleasure of it rather than the misconstrued message that alcohol is good for your health.

The link between the consistent, overconsumption of alcohol and breast cancer is undeniable. Research has shown this time and time again, and for many years now. Yet we rarely hear about it.

The human body cannot excrete alcohol; it has to be converted into acetaldehyde by the liver, and then the acetaldehyde can be excreted. This is the nasty substance that can give us a headache the day after a big night. If the liver didn't do its job properly and alcohol accumulated in our blood, we can go into a coma and die. Alcohol is that poisonous. And I don't say that lightly. But, thankfully, our liver jumps to action and starts the conversion process and we can carry on. Over time, though, this can take its toll.

The trouble is, when we drink daily, or, for some, just regularly, the liver can be so busy dealing with alcohol as its priority, that other substances that the liver has to change so they can be excreted don't get any attention and are recycled. Estrogen and cholesterol are two examples. It is often the reabsorption of these substances that leads to their elevated levels in our bodies—and that can lead to health challenges.

If you want to cut back or cut out alcohol for a while, or even if you just want to break your habit of regular drinking, still pour yourself a drink at the time you would normally have a glass of wine, and do what you would normally do. Sit and chat to your partner, make dinner, talk on the phone to a friend. So often we have mentally linked the glass of wine to a pleasurable activity when it is actually the pleasurable activity that we don't want to miss out on! So have sparkling water in a wine glass, with some fresh lime or lemon if that appeals, and add a few more alcohol free days to your life.

It's time for some liver love! Here's how to recognize signs and symptoms that the liver needs support—and some solutions.

- Liver roll—that increased roll of fat high up under the bra of women, under the pectorals of men.

- Tender point in the center of your torso (can indicate gall bladder issues, heartbreak, or massive disappointment); if your gall bladder has been removed, your liver has to make the bile the gall bladder once did, so additional liver support is often required.

- Very short fuse or temper.

- Episodes or feelings of intense anger.

- "Liverish," gritty, impatient behavior.

- PMS.

- Cellulite (lymphatic also).

- Overheating easily.

- "Floaters" in your vision.

- Waking around 2:00 am

- Sleep which is worse on an evening you consume alcohol.

- Waking hot in the night.

- Not hungry for breakfast when you first get up in the morning.

- Prefer to start your day with coffee.

- Elevated cholesterol.

- Estrogen-dominance symptoms.

- Bloat easily.

- Drinking alcohol daily.

- Daily long-term caffeine consumption.

SOLUTIONS FOR YOUR LIVER

Set yourself a time-based goal when it comes to making these changes. For example, "I will only drink alcohol on weekends for four weeks," or "I will only drink coffee when I go out for breakfast on Sundays."

- Take a break from alcohol.

- Only drink on weekends; no alcohol during the week.

- Replace coffee with green or white tea (or, less often, weak, black tea).

- Support the liver with herbs such as:
  - St Mary's Thistle, especially if alcohol is a regular part of your life
  - Globe artichoke, especially of you have a tendency to constipation and/or a liver roll and/or central torso tenderness

- Bupleurum, especially if there are clots in the menstrual blood

- Schisandra, especially for its detox action (it also works on the adrenals)

- Transform anger into passion by giving a different meaning to a past experience; the energy of anger and passion are the same.

- Drink vegetable juice or a "green smoothie" each morning.

- Snack on seeds and nuts.

- Eat less fruit; none after morning tea.

- Cut out dairy products for a four-week trial and/or

- Cut out grains (containing gluten) for a four-week trial.

- Take an essential fatty acid supplement; a good quality, decent dose of fish oil for reducing cholesterol, or a flax oil, evening primrose combination.

- Eat high zinc foods such as oysters (from clean waters) or take a zinc supplement of zinc picolinate 15 to 30 mg per day and best taken at night just before bed to maximize absorption.

Remember, it is what you do every day that impacts your health, not what you do sometimes. Just get honest with yourself. And take such good care of yourself that your quality of life is forever excellent. We only have one liver.

Gut Bacteria
Puzzle Piece 5

This chapter is relatively brief and to the point as far as fat burning is concerned. It is all about the bacterial species that inhabit your large intestine. It is an area in which I have had intense interest since completing my PhD, part of which involved analyzing fecal samples from children with autism spectrum disorder (ASD). Not really something to discuss at a dinner party!

What my research taught me was that the way we eat influences the species of gut bacteria that inhabit our colon. These bacteria eat and produce waste just as a human does. I explored digestion in the first section of the book, but this chapter is all about the colon and the bugs.

THE CONNECTION BETWEEN GUT BACTERIA AND CALORIES

First, let's explore the influence gut bacteria have over the effect of calories on our body. Wonderful research from 2006 scientifically demonstrated what I had observed in my clients and what countless clients already felt to be true—and that is that there seem to be times in our lives when calories behave as if they are worth more in our body. The research took two groups of genetically identical mice with sterile guts; that is there were no bacteria inhabiting their intestines. The researchers inoculated one group with a range of bacterial species that broadly fit under the name Firmicutes, while the other species were inoculated with Bacteroidetes. Both groups of mice were given an identical number of calories from identical food sources, and (drum roll please!) the group who received the Bacteroidetes species remained the same weight and size while the Firmicutes group gained weight. The mice almost looked "puffy" and "swollen" in the images presented in the scientific paper. This was the first research to show that the types of gut bacteria present in the large bowel may influence the value of calories.

The results of this work went on to be replicated in humans. This study found that people categorized as obese for the purpose of the research had significantly fewer Bacteroidetes in their bowel than lean people in the study. Lean people had a dominance of Bacteroidetes.

Are you one of those people who feels like you only have to look at food for it to end up sticking to you? Do you notice what the people around you eat and wonder how you can be the size you are when you feel as if you eat like a bird? Do you feel the way you eat does not warrant your size? As you have already read in this book, there may be numerous factors at play in this scenario, such as elevated cortisol, estrogen dominance, liver congestion, and/ or excess calories (eating too much for physical or emotional needs). The species of bacteria in your large bowel can also play a role.

When I ask people to change their diets for a period of time, usually an initial four weeks, one of the questions in my head is how do I alter this person's gut bacterial profile so their energy improves, their appetite changes (if they overeat in the first place), and their clothes get looser? The first step is to starve the "bad" bugs.

Just like humans, gut bacteria have food preferences, and they have specific "nutritional" requirements. Guess what they thrive on? Sugar! This gives you the biggest reason ever to eliminate refined sugar from your diet for a minimum of four weeks. Not just reduce it. Eliminate it. You must frame it in your head as four tiny weeks out of your big long life. This small chunk of time may provide you with an extraordinarily important answer to your health issues. If such a challenge feels unattainable, a client who began seeing me when she was 310 pounds (she volunteered to share her weight), taught me a very effective way to do it. After hearing me speak at a seminar, she identified sugar as her biggest challenge. Cutting sugar back, let alone cutting it out completely, seemed impossible to her and felt like an overwhelming task. She's heard me bark on and on about the enormous importance of greens (green vegetables, especially green leaves), and so instead of starting by cutting sugar out, she simply ate more greens. Within four weeks, she no longer even wanted sugar. Her words to me were "it tastes terrible, and I feel like I'm poisoning myself." Extreme perhaps, but you get the message—sugar tastes bad after you've been eating a lot of green foods for a while, because greens are bitter, and the sugar tastes sickeningly sweet. So up your greens, and watch the sugar fall away. Cutting it out of your diet will change your whole chemistry, as you will see in the chapter about alkalinity.

IRRITABLE BOWEL SYNDROME

While I am presenting information about gut bacteria, I want to touch on irritable bowel syndrome (IBS), because a bloated stomach, even though it's different from a fat stomach, can communicate the same message to a brain, particularly to a female one. And studies suggest IBS affects approximately 70 percent of women in the Western world.

WITH A FAT TUMMY, LOGIC DISAPPEARS

Regardless of your physical size, if you look down and see a bloated stomach, there is an alarm that screeches inside your head, whether you recognize it or not, "Look how fat you are!" It doesn't matter if you have eaten healthy food that day and exercised, or eaten poorly and done nothing but sit on your bottom, but if you distinctly recall waking that morning with your tummy looking quite okay but now it looks like you've swallowed a football, then it's going to have an effect. Logic disappears at this point. If you were still thinking logically, you would tell yourself that it is not possible to gain a football's worth of fat in a day and that your tummy is simply bloated, to calm down, things will be fine again in the morning, and that it would be good to get to the bottom of your bloatedness. But the potential for that train of thought left the building the moment your brain saw your protruding tummy.

Instead, common reactions in the psyche, especially the female one, might be sudden onset of a really bad mood, overreaction to anything and everything, tears at the drop of a hat, withdrawal, or a major "what the heck" food attack that leaves the pantry bare! Some people are aware of what led to their change in mood. Most are not. And it is worse for those who have been making massive efforts with food and movement. The people who have eaten poorly that day still feel lousy about themselves, but they follow that lousy feeling with thoughts that drive more lousy feelings such as, "Well, what did you expect? You ate chocolate when you said you weren't going to. You're so hopeless, you have no willpower, and you'll never change." Really non-uplifting sentiments!

Such reactions raise numerous issues, many of which are emotional and are explored in the chapter on emotions. However, on a physical level, which is my focus here, it is essential that we examine why your tummy keeps bloating. Ask yourself:

- Is it related to your menstrual cycle only?

- Does it only happen after you eat lunch? If so, what are you eating for lunch?

- Does your tummy bloat only after an afternoon snack? What are you choosing at this time of day?

- Is it worse when you are stressed? Did it only begin after you went through a great deal of change, positive or not so positive? Did it begin (but perhaps not immediately) after a relationship break up?

- Did it start after an episode of food poisoning or after a holiday where you had a very upset tummy?

My experience with the above scenarios follows.

Menstrual cycle-related bloat

If your tummy only bloats in the lead-up to your period, it is likely to be caused by estrogen dominance. Take the steps outlined in the solutions section of the sex hormones chapter.

After meal bloating

In my experience working with clients I have learned that there are some foods that are better eaten on an empty stomach. Fruit is one of them. If bloating is an issue for you, only eat fruit first thing in the morning on an empty stomach. None for lunch and none mid-afternoon. This includes dried fruit. You may find the same thing happens with starchy carbohydrates such as bread. Some people bloat no matter what time of day they eat bread, and, if that is the case, they will usually do well omitting all gluten-containing grains for a four-week period. Others are fine with bread/toast for breakfast but for lunch it is a disaster in their digestive system.

All foods containing casein (foods derived from an udder; cow, goat, or sheep, although the latter two tend to be tolerated better than cow's milk) can be significant contributors to a bloated stomach. Remove all sources from your diet for a trial period of four weeks and observe how you feel. You will like this next bit even less. Coffee can be incredibly bloating for some people. With a milk-based coffee, it may be the cow's milk or, less often, the soy milk, but even black coffee will cause some people to bloat. Biochemically, coffee drives both liver and gallbladder action, plus it triggers the adrenals to secrete adrenalin, that can go on to affect another adrenal hormone, called aldosterone, which determines how much fluid your body retains. Switch to herbal tea or green tea, and give coffee a rest for four weeks. Green tea still has some caffeine (about one-third the caffeine of coffee) in it, but the effects are buffered by another substance in green tea called theanine. Green tea is also packed with antioxidants and what are believed to be powerful anticancer properties.

Observation is key to this process since your body does not have a voice. Instead it communicates through symptoms and lets you know when it is happy or not. A food that bloats you is, in that moment, not your friend, and your body is simply letting you know. Do not let your head run away with you when you notice this. Remind yourself that just because it bloats you today does not mean you will never eat that food or drink that drink again. It simply means that right now, in this moment, it does not serve you. So take a four-week break from whatever you suspect. No tears, no tantrums, just cut it out for four weeks. You will feel so different when you feed your body precisely what it wants. Never waste a bloated tummy. Ask it what it wants to tell you, as silly as that may sound. Your body has a wonderful wisdom.

Bloated since a stressful experience

If your tummy changed after a challenging time in your life, it is quite likely that your bloated abdomen was initially due to poor stomach acid production. Now, however, if poor stomach acid production has been ongoing because of an almost low-grade (or high-grade) anxiety inside you, the changes in digestion that were initially caused by poor stomach acid production will have changed the gut bacteria and hence the pH of the large bowel. Follow the tips in the Digestion section, in particular those about stimulating stomach acid.

Also, return to the section about stress again, and apply the adrenal support techniques described. Very importantly, but challenging at times, do your best to eat in a calm state. And you will also often see an improvement in symptoms if you follow the food recommendations from the after meal bloating section above. If bloating began after heartbreak, ask the discomfort what it wants you to know. You may feel a little odd having a conversation with your tummy, but your body knows the truth, and you might be surprised at the message it has for you.

Bloated since food poisoning episode or upset tummy while traveling

Despite negative stool tests, I have seen this health picture frequently. Where once they had an iron gut, this person now feels like they react to everything. Even if you had forgotten that a gastroenteritis episode began your digestive system challenges, I suggest you:

- Discuss having a *Helicobacter pylori* test with your general practitioner.

- Take an herbal antiparasitic tablet or liquid, even if your stool test came back negative. Be guided by a health professional, but you usually need relatively high doses three times a day, and you need to take them for a two-month period. If a parasite infection is the basis of your ongoing tummy trouble, the natural medicine must be taken for the full two months, as initially only the live parasites are killed by the herbs. As unpleasant as this is to think about, the parasites will have laid eggs in the lining of your bowel, and you want the herbs in your gut at the ready, in order to get rid of them immediately as they hatch.

- Dietary change as outlined in the after meal bloating section above can be very useful in this situation until the gut has healed. What has become known as a "caveman"-style diet (or the Paleolithic diet), that is both milk and grain free can be beneficial. The Specific Carbohydrate Diet (SCD) has also been noted to have excellent results for gut health challenges and to alter gut bacteria profiles.

THE NO GOOD BUG... STREPTOCOCCUS

There is a bacterial species that I must mention, and I dislike it intensely. It is called *streptococcus*, and my experience in the lab, as well as working with people and their health, has taught me that no good comes from this bug.

It is the bug that causes tonsillitis and ear infections. It is often the basis of pneumonia and other respiratory infections. It lives in our sinuses and builds houses around itself so we can't evacuate it easily. It produces many toxins, as well as lactic acid—more acid to add to our already acidic lifestyles and loads. When our heads are full of mucus, especially when we are young, it can be difficult to cough up all of the sputum, and so we cannot help but swallow some. Our stomach acid is supposed to be super acidic enough to sterilize anything bacterial that we swallow, yet, as outlined in the Digestion section, the pH of the stomach is often too high to perform adequate sterilization. So the strep is able to move through the stomach and take up residence wherever it likes. And there it lives, often forever, in our colon.

LEARN TO KNOW YOUR GUT BUGS

As well as being able to categorize gut bacteria into the groups Firmicutes and Bacteroidetes, we can classify them into those that love oxygen, known as aerobes, and those that don't use oxygen, called anaerobes. For good health, of the aerobic flora in our large bowel, 70 to 90 percent need to be *E. coli,* even though the public mindset tends to link this species to poor hygiene. It is believed that "reasonable" health can be maintained as long as there is 5 percent or less of the *streptococcus* species. I have analyzed stool samples from countless people—adults and children—and I have seen aerobic flora counts of streptococcus at 100 percent of the aerobic flora with zero *E. coli,* or, less extremely, I have seen strep counts of 70 percent and *E. coli* of 30 percent.

Mostly due to my work with children with autism, I have seen firsthand that strep is evil. ASD behaviors decrease significantly with less strep in the gut. In adults, strep makes them wet and mucousy mouth-breathers, which pushes their blood chemistry to the acidic end of the spectrum, an aspect of biochemistry that also influences fat burning (discussed in the alkalinity chapter).

Of the bacterial genres of Firmicutes and Bacteroidetes (remembering that Firmicutes are linked to fat storage and the Bacteroidetes to leanness), strep falls into the Firmicute division. So after all of these years of treating strep in the gut of my clients, knowing they would feel better, breathe better, and that their clothes would get looser, what researching this book has shown me is that all along I have been significantly reducing the Firmicute load in the gut of my clients with the dietary changes I suggest. Isn't the body amazing?

SOLUTIONS FOR YOUR GUT BACTERIA

- Apply any or all of the solutions offered in this chapter including herbal parasite treatments, dairy-free diet trials, or *Helicobacter pylori* tests.

- A caveman-style diet is best to change the gut bacterial ratios: plenty of greens, small servings of red meat, chicken, fish (if you eat them), eggs, nuts, seeds. The Specific Carbohydrate Diet can be very helpful; remember to try it with, and then without, dairy products. Use these diets as a trial, not necessarily forever. If you restrict your diet for more than four weeks, you may need to supplement some nutrients.

- You may "know" that grains are not your friends. If so, cut them out for four weeks to so see how you feel.

- Use 100 percent aloe vera juice to start your day as this can help put the very important mucous lining back on the wall of the bowel.

Useful antimicrobial/immune system herbs include:

  o Golden seal

  o Echinacea

  o Barberry

  o Astragalus

  o Olive leaf

  o Chinese wormwood

  o Black walnut

  o Andrographis

- To use these herbs, it is essential that you seek individual advice from a qualified herbalist.

- It is also essential that you use your bowels daily before using antimicrobial herbs, as you want to eliminate the waste easily.

- Explore the use of colon hydrotherapy from an experienced practitioner.

The Thyroid
Puzzle Piece 6

The thyroid gland is a little butterfly shaped gland that sits in your throat area. It makes hormones that play an enormous role in your metabolic rate as well as temperature regulation. Every day of my working life, I meet people who exhibit virtually every symptom of an underactive thyroid, yet their blood test results demonstrate that everything is in the "normal" range. More on "normal" ranges later.

The production of thyroid hormones involves a cascade of signals, and glands other than the thyroid are also involved. This means that if you have a problem with thyroid hormone levels or with debilitating symptoms indicating something is awry with your thyroid function, then it is essential to get to the heart of the matter so treatment can be appropriately targeted.

The thyroid function cascade begins with the hypothalamus, a gland that makes a hormone that sends a signal to the pituitary gland, the tiny gland that sits at the base of your brain, which we've already seen produces hormones involved in menstruation. The pituitary in turn makes a hormone called thyroid stimulating hormone (TSH) that signals the thyroid to make one if its hormones known simply as T4 (thyroxine). T4 is found in the blood in two forms, namely T4 and free T4 (FT4). They are the same hormone, except one is "free" to enter tissues and the other is bound up and unable to enter tissues, which is where the work needs to be done. However, T4 and FT4 are inactive hormones, and must be converted into the active thyroid hormone called T3 (triiodothyronine). It is T3 that drives your metabolic rate and capacity to burn body fat. The flow chart below illustrates the hormonal cascade.

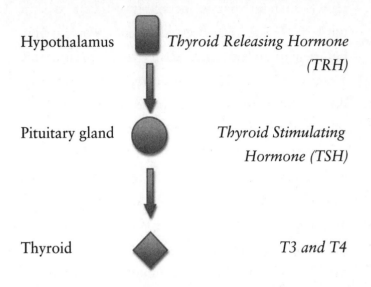

The Thyroid Hormone Cascade:
Signaling begins with the hypothalamus, followed by the pituitary which then in turn signals the thyroid gland to make its hormones.

There are a number of nutrients essential to the production of optimal levels of thyroid hormones. Iodine and selenium are both vital minerals to this process of conversion that literally lights up your metabolic rate! Many people today get very little iodine and selenium in their diets as the majority of soils in the Western world do not contain these trace minerals.

The thyroid gland can become overactive, known as hyperthyroidism, or underactive, known as hypo-thyroidism, and it is the latter scenario that can lead to weight gain that is incredibly difficult to shift until this issue is addressed. Some people swing between an underactive and an overactive situation. The thyroid gland is also susceptible to autoimmune diseases, meaning your immune system, which is supposed to defend you from infection, starts to see the thyroid gland as a foreign particle, like a germ, and attacks it, leading to a change in its function. This can lead to either the overactive picture (with autoimmune involvement this is known as Graves' disease) or an underactive picture (known as Hashimoto's thyroiditis with autoimmune involvement). Infection, poor liver function, iodine, selenium, and iron deficiencies, as well as estrogen dominance or elevated cortisol, are all major factors that can initiate this process. Reread that list and think about what you have already learned from earlier chapters. It is important to work out the path that leads someone to altered thyroid function, for behind the "why" lies most of the answer.

Which factors stand out for you? Sometimes all of the above apply. Never fear, there are solutions.

HYPOTHYROIDISM: UNDERACTIVE THYROID GLAND FUNCTION

Because this book is about explaining what has

to come together for us to be able to burn body fat, I will stay focused on hypothyroidism (underactive thyroid) and what can lead to it. As far as an overactive thyroid goes, I will simply leave it at this: in my experience, stress, specifically the pace of life and what people demand of their body, is the major factor in the development of hyperthyroidism. The people I've worked with who have successfully returned their thyroid function to normal (from being overactive), and had a complete remission of their symptoms, have literally changed their life. They usually change their jobs and, if that is not possible, they completely change their approach and attitude to life. It has been inspiring to witness in my clients. Louise Hay suggests there is a feeling of "rage at being left out," and she encourages people to affirm "I am the center of my life, and I approve of myself and all that I see."

Back to hypothyroidism. The classic symptoms of hypothyroidism are:

- Gradual weight increase over months for no apparent reason
- Often feeling cold, sometimes cold in your bones and like you can't get warm
- Tendency to constipation

- Tendency to depressed mood, forgetfulness, and a sense of being easily confused
- Hair loss or hair drier than previously
- Menstrual problems
- Difficulty conceiving
- Beyond tired, you are fatigued
- Headaches

Let's explore the roads to an underactive thyroid and where to begin to support your thyroid health.

INFECTION & POOR LIVER DETOXIFICATION

A history of glandular fever (Epstein-Barr Virus also know as mononucleosis), for example, is a common road to hypothyroidism, as is liver over-load. Treatment of both of these roads involves taking excellent care of the liver. Apply the liver-loving strategies outlined in the liver chapter. Additionally, Astragalus is an excellent herb to use for a chronic infection background if an herbalist agrees this will meet your needs.

MINERAL DEFICIENCIES

Since hypothyroidism can be influenced by deficiencies in selenium, iodine, and iron—choose foods that are rich in these minerals. Eat brazil nuts daily for selenium. Use Celtic sea salt with iodine and/

or cook with seaweeds such as Kombu for iodine. Good food sources of iron include beef, lamb, eggs, mussels, sardines, lentils, green leafy vegetables, and dates. There is a small amount of iron in many foods, so eating a varied diet is important. And remember that absorption is enhanced by vitamin C. If you do not eat animal foods, do not assume you are iron deficient. For some vegetarians, their body utilizes the iron from vegetables sources very efficiently.

The other option is to take a supplement that covers these nutrients. There are some excellent thyroid support capsules on the market so seek out one of these if it appeals. Regarding iron, it can be good to have a test before you supplement as overloading on iron is not good. But if you are deficient it can be challenging and a very slow process to get your iron levels up without supplementation. So it is good to know your blood levels of this mineral. Many iron supplements are constipating, but most people find this doesn't happen with liquid iron supplements.

Here's some more on Iodine from a magazine article I wrote... just so you know how important this is!

Iodine

Iodine is a trace mineral so essential to our health that our body begins to shut down without it. Our thyroid gland loves iodine, and it cannot make thyroid hormones without it. Symptoms of an underactive thyroid include a deep tiredness and sluggish, heavy feeling; dry skin or hair; feelings of cold; a tendency to be constipated; puffy eyes; and a tendency to a depressed mood. Increasing dietary iodine intake can make a difference.

Thyroid hormones essentially determine our metabolic rate as adults and our growth as children. Iodine is also essential to the IQ of the developing brain *in utero* and, sadly, studies are now showing that some children in the Western world are suffering from such low iodine levels that their IQ is being detrimentally affected.

Why is this so?

Soil is a poor source of iodine, and if a nutrient is not in the soil it cannot be in our food. Where once foods made from whole grains, for example, were good sources in areas where the soil contained iodine in the first place, the depletion of the mineral content of our soils means this is no longer the case. New Zealand, for example, has volcanic soil, which has never contained any iodine. While the soil may not be a good source of iodine, the sea is somewhat better.

Food sources of iodine include all of the seaweeds, which you can add to soups, stews, casseroles, and salads to give them a subtle salty flavor while imparting all of the nutritional value of the minerals. A form of seaweed commonly eaten is nori, used frequently in sushi. Iodine is in small amounts in seafood, but even eating seafood every day will not provide you with adequate amounts of iodine.

Salt was first iodized in 1924; however, it tended to go out of "fashion" with the advent of rock salts and Celtic sea salt. Although Celtic sea salt offers the additional benefits of a broad range of trace minerals, it lacks iodine unless it has been fortified. The only concern with conventional iodized salts is that most brands contain anti-caking agents that are not ideal for human health.

The impact of iodine therapy for the maintenance of healthy breast tissue has been widely reported, although it is rarely discussed. The ovaries also concentrate iodine, and studies have shown that a form of estrogen associated with breast cancer is produced by the ovaries in an iodine-deficient state. This has been shown to be reversible once iodine levels are optimal again.

Iodine is a difficult mineral to test for. Accurate tests require you to collect twenty-four hours of urine, and, remarkably, not all countries offer this testing.

Adult females require 120 micrograms (µg), males 150µg, of iodine per day to prevent deficiency. It is far more beneficial, however, to individualize doses. Often amounts between twelve and fifty milligrams (mg) are initially necessary to treat a deficient state, and this can be easily done with one to three drops of a good quality liquid iodine solution per day, available from some health food shops or through a compounding pharmacist. It is best to obtain specific advice to learn how to meet your individual needs.

ESTROGEN DOMINANCE

Too much estrogen suppresses thyroid function while optimal progesterone levels support its function. Apply the strategies for dealing with estrogen dominance if you suspect that this is the basis for your challenge with your thyroid gland.

ELEVATED CORTISOL BROUGHT ON BY STRESS

Elevated cortisol as a result of stress decreases the levels of the active, fat burning thyroid hormone T3, which slows your metabolism. Added to this, high levels of cortisol urge your body to break down muscle to provide glucose for your brain, and reducing your muscle slows your metabolic rate as well. In the absence of stress, a healthy body converts FT4 into T3, but with elevated cortisol levels, the conversion of FT4 to T3 decreases.

Poor conversion of FT4 to active T3 also occurs

if you restrict your food intake. Your body assumes that you must be starving, and therefore it must slow down the metabolic rate to preserve those precious fat stores! It may be frustrating, but your body's primary goal is always for survival.

Elevated cortisol also inhibits the release of TSH from the pituitary—with less TSH, the body produces less FT4. Apply the strategies for high cortisol outlined in the stress hormones chapter if this scenario rings true for you. Poor thyroid function can also lead to elevated cholesterol, and once thyroid function has been treated, the cholesterol returns to normal.

THYROID MEDICATIONS

Typically today, if someone has been diagnosed with an underactive thyroid, they are prescribed thyroxine (T4). Some people feel brilliant on this medication and all of their hypothyroid symptoms disappear, including their weight gain. If this has not happened for you despite taking this medication, try a different approach! After years of taking thyroxine, it will not suddenly start to work if it hasn't yet.

There are numerous brands of thyroxine on the market. If you want to stick with conventional medicine, tell your general practitioner you feel lousy on your current medication and that you would like to try a different drug. I have hundreds of clients who were happily taking one form of thyroxine and when the thyroid medication that is subsidized was changed to a different brand, all of their symptoms returned. Explore this even if your blood levels of TSH, FT4, and T3 are "normal," but you still have symptoms.

In my opinion, an excellent option when it comes to hypothyroidism is whole thyroid extract (WTE). This is taken instead of any synthetic medication and, unlike the synthetics providing only one of the thyroid hormones, WTE provides all of the thyroid hormones. It is essential that you see your doctor about this and, if you so choose, be guided in the transition from a synthetic to the WTE, which is made by a compounding pharmacist.

If you have not been diagnosed with a thyroid illness, but you exhibit numerous symptoms, do not rely solely on your blood test results to determine if your thyroid is underactive. Work with a health professional who will treat the symptoms, not the blood, and who will monitor both your symptoms and the blood work as you explore treatments. I learned this in a powerful way with a client whose story melts my heart.

The importance of testing thyroid antibodies is best demonstrated with this story. A precious lady arrived at my practice for assistance with her health, and when I asked how I could help, she burst into tears and said she knows she has had an underactive thyroid for about thirty years. Jane's blood tests always come back as normal, and no one would treat her. She had gained over 220 pounds over thirty years, and it all began when her dear mom passed away. Jane said she had eaten poorly for about three to four months after her mom's death, and put on weight, but her grief gradually eased and, as it did, she started to eat better again, as she always had. But nothing changed. Her size kept increasing. So then she didn't just eat well, she signed up for a gym membership, and she started to eat even better. When I saw her, Jane was unable to exercise due to knee pain from carrying so much weight (her description and she thought she was "about 400 pounds"), but she still ate in a way that did not warrant her size.

Of course Jane had a huge amount of unresolved grief, which I will explore later and of course there had been times when she hadn't eaten very well. She had, at times, become incredibly frustrated that despite her efforts nothing would shift. But she had also had plenty of months and years of making extraordinary efforts for no reward.

Given that Jane ticked every box when it came to symptoms of an underactive thyroid, I decided to request fresh blood tests and include thyroid antibodies, specifically thyroid peroxidase and thyroglobulin. Having been taught at university that it was highly unlikely for thyroid antibodies to be elevated and an issue if thyroid hormone levels were in the normal range, I could understand why Jane's autoantibodies had not been tested—but from a symptoms perspective I could not.

To cut a very long story short, despite her latest thyroid hormones levels being in the "normal" range, all but skewed one way (discussed below), Jane's antibodies were the highest I have ever seen. To put this in context, the "normal" range for both antibodies in this national laboratory is less than fifty (<50). Jane's thyroid peroxidase and thyroglobulin were both >6500—off the scale and through the roof. When I phoned her to tell her, she was at first thrilled that all along there had been a reason for how lousy she had felt. She told me later that anger then surfaced for a life she felt she'd missed out on because this was not picked up. She had remained very shy, which she blamed on her size, and on reflection was very sad that she had not met a partner with whom to share her life. She decided to seek out the most natural approach she could for her very underactive thyroid, and after considerable weight fell off her over the first three months, she booked her first overseas holiday. There is always a why. You just have to find it.

BLOOD TESTS AND "NORMAL" RANGES

The concept of a normal range is necessary, as cutoff points help indicate when something may be abnormal. I have great concerns, however, when we base the future of a person's health on blood tests alone.

According to Dr. Karen Coates, an insightful and pioneering general practitioner and co-author of *Embracing The Warrior: An Essential Guide for Women*, the normal range for some blood tests is calculated periodically by each pathology laboratory to ensure that the reference range printed on the test results is "accurate." On the morning of this day, the first 100 blood samples received are tested for their (in this case) TSH levels in order to determine the reference range. Or it might be iron levels for example. But! Why do people usually have blood tests? Because they are feeling particularly spritely that day? No! Most often, the precise opposite is true! Yet it seems we base our "normal" ranges on these figures. Furthermore, it is also important to understand how the "average" amount of a particular nutrient or hormone is calculated. Mathematically, the top reference point is calculated to be "two standard deviations" above the average, while the bottom figure is "two standard deviations" below the average. The arbitrary rules of this method dictate that 95 percent of the 100 blood samples taken must fall into the "normal" range. The statistical definition of standard deviations insists that only four or five results may fall outside this reference range, two samples below and two above.

The two points I want to make are: first, the reference ranges for some blood parameters are getting broader. The normal range for TSH when I wrote the first draft of this book was 0.4 to 4.0. The normal range has since been expanded to 0.3 to 5.0 only four months later. As mentioned later, people at either end of this blood range will look and feel completely different and they will more than likely exhibit thyroid symptoms. If they are symptom free, no problem, but my concern is this: if we base treatment on the blood work alone and leave people to live with their symptoms with their result skewed to one end of the normal range, we are risking, not optimizing, their health. This brings me to my next point, which is that you can see from the start that this process is flawed, given it is done on individuals who are unwell. It is more challenging to create optimal health, prevent disease, and maximize quality of life for people when they are being guided with their blood tests to fall into a potentially unhealthy normal range.

YOUR BLOOD TESTS

I urge you to get copies of your own blood tests and look for results being skewed to one end of the normal range. Let me explain.

The normal range for TSH where I live is 0.3 to 5.0. Although those numbers may seem small, someone with a TSH of 0.3 feels and looks completely different from someone with a TSH of 5. Additionally, if your results are not actually outside the normal range, you will usually be told (well-meaningly) that there is no problem with your thyroid. A common picture I see is a TSH of 2.5 or greater screaming out to the thyroid gland to make FT4. FT4 normal levels are ten to twenty and usually, for someone with symptoms of hypothyroidism, their FT4 will be eleven. This person feels exhausted, has trouble naturally using their bowels daily, has dry skin, very low motivation, brain fog, and their clothes are gradually getting tighter. Their thyroid needs support.

In this case, I always start with iodine and selenium

and sometimes iron, along with adrenal support, a grain-free diet, and a big chat about their beliefs and what their perception is of what life is like for them. Louise Hay teaches that thyroid problems represent feelings and beliefs around humiliation and feeling like you never get to do what you want to do (how many mothers does that describe?!?). Louise Hay suggests someone with thyroid problems unconsciously asks, "when is it going to be my turn?" She suggests you develop a new thought pattern of "I move beyond old limitations and now allow myself to express freely and creatively." Underneath diagnosed hypothyroidism, Louise Hay suggests, are feelings of hopelessness, a feeling of being stifled, and a sense of giving up. She suggests you develop a new thought pattern of "I create a new life with new rules that totally support me."

I include this information to offer you a whole picture of your thyroid health, from the conventional function of hormones and glands and blood tests; through the nutritional supports that are essential, including iodine and selenium; to the metaphysical. Somewhere among these three approaches lies your answer, not necessarily in one or the other. I urge you to explore all three.

Solutions are scattered throughout this chapter, so please go back and reread it a second time to create your plan of action to optimize thyroid function.

My additional suggestions are:

- Go on a grain-free diet trial for a minimum of four weeks.

- If you *love* dairy products and the idea of going without cheese makes you wonder if you could, then do it! It is often what we love (not just like) to eat that can be a problem. Do a four-week dairy free trial if this is the case.

- Support liver and gallbladder function to assist with bowel elimination. Globe artichoke is particularly good for "thyroid" people.

- Refer to the advice about estrogen dominance.

- Adrenal support is almost essential, especially when beginning to treat the thyroid. Refer to the stress hormones chapter to refresh on adrenal support strategies.

- You will probably crave coffee. Please explore taking a four-week break and observe how you feel at the end of this period. Use green tea, which has a low caffeine level, instead.

- If you have a diagnosed thyroid condition and you are on synthetic medication but your symptoms are still present, explore transitioning to whole thyroid extract under medical supervision.

Insulin
Puzzle Piece 7

The pancreas is another gland (technically it is a "gland organ") that makes a hormone intricately linked to body-fat burning or accumulation. Insulin is made by the pancreas, and it is a type of growth hormone, hence its capacity to drive fat storage. We make insulin when we eat. Carbohydrates elicit the largest production while protein drives only a small amount of insulin release, which is usually offset by another hormone that protein elicits called glucagon that acts in the opposite way to insulin. People have become confused about and fearful of carbs, yet it's imperative that we consume some carbohydrates since they are vital to the function of our brain, kidneys, and red blood cells. So how do we optimize carbohydrate intake while still burning fat?

HOW CARBS CAN MAKE YOU FAT—OR NOT

When you consume carbohydrates, whether they are starchy or sweet carbs, they are broken down into glucose. Sources of carbohydrates include bread, pasta, rice, all types of potatoes, and the other starchy vegetables (including pumpkin and corn), fruit, dairy products, candy, cakes, cookies, pastries, honey, maple syrup, and sugar. I have found it fascinating to ask audiences to shout out sources of carbohydrates. Today, the only carbs audiences tend to identify are the starches (bread and potato are the first two words out of their mouths every time), which I believe is the result of the high protein diet era. Eleven years ago, when I asked audiences to name sources of carbs, the first and almost only word out of their mouths was sugar. Back then, fat was still the "enemy" of the public health nutrition messages, and the public believed that as long as there was very little fat in a food, then it had to be good. Bread and pasta are high in what were known as complex carbohydrates and very low in fat, and people ate them by the bucket load. Back then, there was still some wariness about sugar, as it had been hailed as the only enemy in the late 1970s on the back end of the previous high-protein diet age. You see, nutrition information moves in cycles, and it will continue to do so. To avoid getting caught in the latest fad, I remind you that nature gets it right, and it is human intervention that makes food less nourishing and sustaining. My point here is that starch-based foods are carbs but so is anything that tastes sweet, unless it has been flavored by artificial sweeteners (see comment later in this chapter) or stevia, a beautiful sweet herb.

This glucose from the carbohydrates ends up in your blood stream, and your body identifies that blood sugar levels have been elevated. Your body does not like it when blood glucose goes high, as too much sugar in the blood can damage the lining of the blood vessels, in a similar way to a free radical (described in the Liver chapter). To protect the blood vessels from damage, the pancreas secretes insulin into the blood. It is the job of insulin to remove the excess glucose from the blood so that homeostasis (balance) returns to the blood. As you will see in more detail in the alkalinity chapter, the health and happiness of the blood must be maintained at all costs.

Insulin first takes the sugar to the muscles and

the liver, where it is stored as glycogen, places from which it can be released easily if we need a fast source of energy if we haven't eaten for a while. But the size of our muscles is finite, meaning they have their storage limit. Once they are full of glycogen, if more sugar from the blood needs to be removed, then insulin will transport it to guess where? The fat cells. Fat cells have an infinite capacity to expand.

An essential point to make here is that our muscle mass is critical. Do not allow yourself to lose muscle from this point forward in your life. At best, increase your muscle mass. At least, maintain it where it is today. Given the glycogen storage capacity of muscles and the ready source of energy they offer, coupled with the metabolism driving power of muscles, I cannot encourage you enough to grow them! You do not need to become a body builder. You do not need to lift huge amounts of weight. I suggest you focus on strengthening the muscles housed in your core. Of course you can also work on the pretty ones that everyone can see, but make sure your core gets attention. Think about this. All of your organs that keep you alive, other than your brain, are housed inside your torso. These organs are held in place by muscles. Over time, due to gravity and poor lifestyle choices, these muscles want to go south and, when this happens, they no longer work as efficiently as they once did. Pilates, yoga, and qi gong are all excellent for core strength, and you can sometimes even activate your core while walking for a little extra bonus.

FOOD AND INSULIN

Exploring the human history of food helps guide us with what to eat, especially when it comes to managing insulin levels. The only carbohydrates humans once ate were legumes, pulses (eg. lentils), and berries. These days, there are over 3000 snack food items alone on the average supermarket's shelves, and this number is growing constantly. None of these packaged foods are what I call "low human intervention" (low HI) foods. Even white bread looks nothing like the stalk of wheat from which it came. If you showed a four-year-old a stalk of wheat and a piece of white bread, do you think that four-year-old could tell you that the stalk of wheat made the white bread? Unlikely, as they are not even the same color. That stalk of wheat has been bleached, rolled, and pummeled to create that piece of white bread, so much so that all of the nutrition that was present in the original stalk of wheat has been removed and, for that slice of white bread to have any goodness at all, the nutrients have to be added back synthetically. And just as an aside, how did you make glue when you were at school? With flour and water. Now, they package it up and sell it to us. I am not saying don't ever eat white bread. If you love it, buy it fresh from a good quality baker, who uses no preservatives, perhaps on a Saturday morning, or better still, buy it fortnightly or monthly and enjoy it. Remember, it is what you do every day that has the greatest impact on your health, not what you do sometimes. If you love it, eat it. Just not bucket loads and not every day. And if you need to have a four-week break from grains because of an inkling you might have got from information earlier in this book, then take your break and bring it back on occasions if you want to.

It is big surges of insulin on and off over the day or constantly high circulating insulin that cause the problem when it comes to fat burning. If you have spent months committed to exercising and eating well with little or no reward, have your blood glucose level as well as your blood insulin level tested. I have had clients with perfect blood glucose levels but their bodies are making huge amounts of insulin to keep their blood glucose inside the normal range, and you never know this until you test the insulin. No matter how much you exercise or how seemingly amazingly you eat, you will not access your fat stores to burn in this biochemical state. Insulin must be addressed.

A typical pattern of food intake that I witness regularly is this: You get up in the morning, inhale some sort of processed breakfast cereal, and race out the door to work. Your blood sugar soars, and your pancreas subsequently releases a surge of insulin. *Welcome to fat storage situation number one of your day.* You take shallow breaths all morning due to the perceived pressures in your day. After your peak in blood sugar from your cereal, by midmorning, your blood sugar plummets, and concentration levels are waning. You are relieved when you look at your watch at 10:30 a.m. You haven't achieved very much in your day until now other than trying to get on top of emails that you actually never seem to get on top of, but at least 10:30 means it is time for a break, an opportunity to get away from your desk, either with colleagues or by yourself, and head to the nearest coffee cart or café. You justify your desire, and subsequent purchase of a muffin, along with your large double shot skinny milk latte, by telling yourself that you have a big day ahead and you'll probably go to the gym later anyway. *Welcome to fat storage situation part two of your day.*

You return to your desk and push on with some work, but, after about one-and-a-half to two hours, you are fidgety again and want lunch. Your blood sugar has come down from its high brought on by your midmorning snack. You look at your watch again… thank goodness! It's lunch time! And out you go for lunch. You know you feel better in your tummy on days when you don't eat bread for lunch, but you tell yourself that you are busy and you need to be quick. A sandwich, bagel, or a roll is always quick and easy. You inhale it. Then you want something sweet. Hmmm. Chocolate? No, not yet. Fruit. Okay, good choice, you think. And, on the inside, your blood sugar and consequently your insulin level surge again. *Welcome to fat storage situation number 3*. Within half an hour, you feel utterly exhausted, probably bloated, and you are berating yourself because you feel fat. You are, in fact, simply bloated but your discomfort and the wind building in your tummy, coupled with your "fat" abdomen makes you feel gross. You work in an open-plan office, so you are conscious of hanging on to that wind in case it has an odor. And so even though your colleagues may be (unknowingly) grateful, the bloating and hence the size of your tummy increases over the afternoon.

HEADSPACE AND HORMONES

The psychological process that goes on in your

head, particularly if you are a woman, after lunch when you reflect on what you have consumed that morning, is incredibly detrimental to your health and your cortisol levels and, hence, your waistline. You feel like all you did was eat all morning and sit on your bottom. You think about the dress you were planning to fit into to wear to an event three weeks from now. Even though all you have done is eat breakfast, a muffin, a coffee, and a roll, in that moment, you believe that you will never fit into that dress and even though you thought you would go to the gym that evening, having not achieved very much over your morning, you know you will work late and not go. You think about the gym membership that cost you half a month's pay and that you haven't used it for the last three months, and you feel useless. You think again about the "massive" (as perceived by you) amounts of food you have eaten so far that day, and you hate yourself and your swollen abdomen. Then! Light bulb! A thought that suddenly makes you feel better flashes into your mind. You suddenly feel back in control. What was that thought? "I'll skip that afternoon snack!"! You feel better, because you have found a way out of your perceived eating frenzy and expanding (bloated) waistline. But your blood sugar and insulin picture over your morning resembled a roller coaster, and how do you expect your blood sugar picture to be any different than it was in the morning? The answer is it won't be. By 3:00 to 4:00 p.m., your blood sugar has plummeted again, and you feel exhausted. The momentary elation from your "no afternoon tea" thought has vaporized, and you are now "starving" to the point that you could eat your arm off. Your blood *sugar* is rock bottom. So, instinctively, what type of food do you think your body will desperately want you to eat? You guessed it. Sugar. Almost nothing raises your blood sugar faster, and your biochemical drive for survival knows it. And now you feel so desperate for it, nothing is going to stand in your way. But if you give in and you eat something, when you said you wouldn't, what emotion do you feel? G-U-I-L-T, guilt. And what stress hormone do you think guilt drives your body to make? C-O-R-T-I-S-O-L, cortisol. What a vicious cycle.

So you give in and you eat whatever sweet fix you can lay your hands on. Some women will placate the need for food at this time by having their second coffee for the day. There's no way a black coffee would hit the spot at this time of day. Those who choose the coffee option feel mildly pleased because they didn't give in and eat—but then these people "know" in the back of their mind that a second coffee is not ideal for them either. New clients express precisely this to me every day of my working life. But they console themselves with "at least I didn't eat." Those who do eat feel momentarily better with yet another elevation in blood sugar and consequently insulin. *And hello fat storage situation number 4 for the day.* Then the self-directed cruel statements silently begin. "You are hopeless. You have no willpower. Look at your stomach." It is the "will I, won't I, I said I wouldn't, but I did" syndrome (WIWIISIWBID syndrome or more simply the BID syndrome). And in that mindset, you're still at your desk at 6:30 pm, still trying to get on top of the work you didn't do that day because you were so busy thinking about food and exercise and dresses and your stomach and not passing gas, that you *can't* go to the gym now because it is already 6:30 pm. You still have more work to do, and if you work until 7:15 pm, well, there's no food at home so you will have to go to the supermarket, but, if you go to the supermarket, it will be 8:00 pm before you get home and then you still have to chop the vegetables, and that takes ages. And then you still have to cook, eat, and clean up, so it will be at least 11:30 pm before you are finished doing all of that, and you probably need to do more work at home that night. But you have to wash your hair in the morning and then straighten it and so you need to get up earlier to do that...

And then you get up and do it all over again, and you wonder why you can't lose weight when you don't eat "that badly." I know I used a similar scenario earlier, but it seemed appropriate here as well—and it is a pattern common to many, many women. I call it Rushing Woman Syndrome (RW Syndrome for ease of expression). Although I may have exaggerated some of the details of the scenario above—or not really!—and there are many variations to what I have described, which may include children, partners, parents, or friends, I meet women of all ages who live like this and also some men.

There may or may not be big, traumatic stresses going on, but there is a daily, relentless juggling act that never ends. Such a scenario is typical of adults between the ages of twenty-five and sixty-five, although it tends to be far more prominent in those between the ages of thirty and fifty-five. It comes from a desire to be all things to all people, from being a "pleaser" in your nature, behavior that was rewarded in childhood. It makes people like you, and you feel good helping out and being there for others, but you never, ever put yourself first. You are exhausted and, if you don't feel that way, you are usually living on adrenaline.

The cocktail of hormones being made in the BID and the RW syndromes mostly involves cortisol and insulin. This disastrous cocktail in turn interferes with progesterone production, so estrogen becomes dominant. This down-regulates thyroid function, so you drink coffee or wine, or both, to speed up and cool down respectively each day—and your liver gets a regular thumping. And still no one eats enough green food. Throw in some emotional confusion and chaos, still to be addressed, and you have *Accidentally Overweight*. Can you now see why I suggested earlier in this book that it is never about the food—but yet on the other hand, it is *all* about the food? It's time to slow down.

HOW THE BIOCHEMISTRY OF INSULIN RELATES TO APPETITE AND FAT STORAGE

Please understand that through this entire book I am not suggesting that we are not responsible for how much and what we eat. We are 100 percent responsible for this. Nor am I saying that willpower plays no role. Of course it can. My concern is that many people view food, weight, fat, and size simply as components of calories in versus calories burnt equation, and they believe that if you eat anything other than what you know to be healthy, then you are useless. What I simply want to point out to the world is that our hormones are powerful, and your drive for safety and survival overrides everything.

Regardless of how frustrated you may be with your ever- expanding size, take the time to explore your whys. Which hormones identified in this book so far stand out to you? Do you think that you eat emotionally? Read on to learn more about the power and interrelationships of insulin.

Over the past thirty or so years, what has become known as the "obesity epidemic" has unfolded. People tend to judge others and assume they must eat too much and move too little, and there are times when this is accurate. Judgment is explored in the chapter on emotions. But what I want to explore with you now, however, is—what is it about the physiology of the human body that is allowing this to happen? Our biochemistry has what are called built-in negative feedback mechanisms that are supposed to stop us from gaining too much weight. In some people, this is not working efficiently or, if it is, it is being ignored biochemically. Scientists have been exploring what has the ability to block these signals that are supposed to tell our body to eat less and move more. Clearly, something is getting in the way. And most research indicates that insulin is precisely this block. The entire role of insulin is to store energy, and, in a world of plenty, in a world full of processed carbs, because insulin does its job, we gain weight.

As described earlier, insulin moves glucose out of

the blood and into the muscles and fat cells, which results in the weight increase. But regardless of size—although this scenario tends to be more distinct in very overweight people—if insulin levels are high, another hormone called leptin is supposed to kick in and tell your brain that you've eaten. Leptin is produced by fat in the fat cells, and circulates through the blood, binding to receptors in the hypothalamus, the area of the brain that controls energy balance. Leptin is supposed to turn off the desire to eat. In addition to this, it also triggers the involvement of the autonomic nervous system, various parts of which either promote or block fat burning. Through research that involved suppressing insulin with a drug, it has been shown that insulin interferes with leptin's ability to signal the brain to stop eating. However, studies in which leptin was given to obese people under the hypothesis that it would shut off appetite have usually found that it is not the miracle pill it was anticipated to be. It appears that insulin stops your brain from being able to "see" leptin, which leaves leptin lousy at down-regulating appetite. The key here is that insulin must first come down for appetite to decrease, especially the desire for carbohydrates, and for weight loss to be sustained.

Resistance exercise is essential and the best "drug" of all for dealing with insulin. We are crazy if we think exercise only works through burning calories. Twenty minutes of jogging = one chocolate chip cookie. One Big Mac = three hours of vigorous exercise to "work it off." The reasons behind the importance of exercise are far beyond burning calories.

Firstly, exercise increases the sensitivity of skeletal muscle to insulin. In other words, exercise makes your muscles more insulin sensitive. When this happens your pancreas can make less insulin, so your levels of insulin will decrease. And the result will be less insulin in your blood to turn sugar into fat. The second reason that movement is important is because, after diaphragmatic breathing, certain types of exercise are the single best "treatments" to lower cortisol, your chronic stress hormone. More on this in a moment. Cortisol lays down what is known as "bad" visceral fat, the fat around the middle, stored so your body will always have energy to escape from the danger (real or perceived) and to keep you alive. By reducing cortisol you are decreasing the amount of fat that gets deposited around your middle, and this also inadvertently reduces your food intake.

FRUCTOSE AND THE LIVER: THEIR RELATIONSHIP TO INSULIN

An excess of any food or beverage over time can make you lay additional body fat down. But there are some that need to be looked at in more detail. One—fructose—is a dietary component well worth discussing when it comes to insulin.

Fructose is the carbohydrate found naturally in foods such as fruit, corn, and honey. The trouble is human consumption of fructose has significantly escalated over the past thirty years, as it has been added to more and more processed foods. Our bodies are simply not designed to consume so much of it. Most people (unless you are excluding fruit to see if it decreases your bloating) can handle two pieces of fruit per day and some honey in tea. There is usually no problem with this, except in specific health conditions, relating mainly to liver and/or gut health. Fruit, honey, and corn themselves are nourishing foods. Please hear this. It is the *over-consumption* of fructose that is the problem. American statistics suggest that the consumption of fructose has gone from less than half a pound per year (about 250 grams) a year in 1970 to 56 pounds (twenty-five kilograms) per year in 2003, an enormous escalation caused by a massive increase in the consumption of processed foods.

Originally, fructose was used in food products for people with diabetes; it has a low glycaemic index (GI), meaning it is digested slowly so drives a very modest insulin response. Researchers had suggested that fructose was not actually regulated by insulin and, therefore, it was presented to the world as the "perfect sugar for people with diabetes." High fructose corn syrup (HFCS) came on the market after it was invented in 1966, and it began to find its way into American foods in 1975. In 1980, soft drink companies started to introduce it into soft drinks. Research suggests that the prevalence of childhood obesity in America can be traced back to this shift. Even though the chemistry of fat burning is multi-faceted, wide-spread use of HFCS certainly hasn't helped and has added dramatically to the road-blocks to fat burning.

The difference with fructose is not the number of calories per gram. In this respect, it is no different than ordinary table sugar. The biggest difference is that the only organ in your body that can actually take up fructose is your liver. The body cannot use fructose for energy; it must first be broken down into its simplest form, and an enzyme the liver makes is essential for this process. Glucose, on the other hand, can be taken up by every organ, and only about 20 percent of your glucose load arrives at your liver. The fewer loads on the liver, the better! It is important to note, however, that sucrose (table sugar) is made up of glucose and fructose, so sucrose also places an additional load on the liver particularly due to its fructose content.

The excessive consumption of fructose has been shown to do three not so great things within the liver; in fact fructose has been shown to be a hepato-toxin ("hepato" meaning liver). First, it drives the liver to make additional uric acid, the accumulation of which causes gout. It has also been suggested that elevated uric acid is the basis of some forms of high blood pressure. Uric acid inhibits nitric oxide, which is one of the body's natural blood pressure lowering agents. Second, excess fructose consumption initiates what is called, in scientific circles, *de novo lipogenesis*, meaning "new fat synthesis," which can lead to problems with blood fats and the ratio of cholesterol and triglycerides (free fat) in the blood. And, third, it appears that excessive consumption of fructose can drive inflammation in the liver, which appears to stop the liver's insulin receptors from working. When this happens, insulin levels throughout the entire body rise, so even though we link insulin to blood glucose and the pancreas—since that is where it is made—you can also see how blood sugar dysregulation and/or insulin resistance is related to liver function. I say it again: we must look after our liver! The effects of elevated insulin are actually systemic.

As you now know, when insulin levels rise, they tell every cell of your body to store fat, and they can interfere with normal brain metabolism of the insulin signal, which is linked to leptin (as described above). If you put all of this together, elevated insulin not only leads to increased body fat but also to increased fat in the liver and the liver driving more body deposition of fat as well as increased inflammation. My goodness! What you end up with is a non-alcoholic fatty liver, which some suggest will soon be considered a disease. When this is going on, your brain can't receive the signal from leptin to stop eating, so you consume more (usually carbs). What a vicious cycle! Imagine if you threw in a few alcoholic drinks each week on top of that chemical chaos! And so many people do. It is not surprising so many people feel lousy. In America, soft drinks and many processed foods, such as pretzels, contain high fructose corn syrup, which is either 42 or 55 percent fructose. In Australia and New Zealand, soft drinks and most of what I call "birthday party" foods contain sucrose. Sucrose (table sugars) is 50 percent fructose (the rest is glucose), so both are a huge worry. Ouch, our livers!

Before you panic and go to a dietary extreme that humans are so good at, usually to their long term detriment, remind yourself that fructose, when combined with fiber, such as naturally occurs in fruit, is far better for us (obviously) than cakes, cookies, and candy. For example, an average-sized orange has twenty calories, ten of which are fructose, and it is high in fiber. A glass of orange juice has 126 calories. It takes 6 oranges to make that glass of juice, and it contains zero fiber. Dietary fiber is important because it slows the rate of intestinal carbohydrate absorption, which in itself reduces the insulin response.

Do your best to choose foods as you would find them in nature. Don't be a fruit bat and eat eight pieces a day. Two is perfect or, as I said earlier, zero for a four-week trial to get on top of bloating. If you eliminated fruit and are reintroducing it, bring it back first on an empty stomach, and see how you tolerate it. Remember, one aspect of exploring your health is about giving you answers to pain, feelings, discomfort, or even illness in your body; four weeks of dietary changes may provide you with some insight. It is up to you to decide what you do with your new information. Truly caring about yourself is paramount, and the chapter about emotions will reveal a new way of doing this.

The glycaemic index (GI) is the response of your blood glucose to fifty grams of carbohydrate in that food. It comes from research that was pioneered at the University of Sydney in Australia, and it changed the face of treatment for Type 1 and Type 2 diabetes, which are in fact biochemically two very different conditions. A food can be classed as low GI because it makes your blood sugar rise very slowly, causing only a small amount of insulin (fat storage hormone) to be secreted. On the other hand, a carbohydrate that is digested quickly causes blood sugar to rise quickly, requiring insulin and hence fat storage signals to surge.

In my opinion, the GI is a very small part of this picture. I prefer to talk about choosing foods that are low HI—low human intervention. Nature knows best. Furthermore, what is now known as the glycaemic load (GL) has come to be shown as a far better guide when it comes to foods, if we need a guide other than nature. Take carrots for example. Carrots are very high GI. If you eat 50 grams of carbohydrate in carrots (please note, that does not mean 50 grams total of carrots, it is referring to 50 grams of the carbs in carrots as they contain other substances such as fiber and water), your blood sugar goes up very high; hence it is a high GI food. Fructose, on the other hand is a low GI food. Soft drinks in the U.S. have a GI of 53, which is low, but this is because it is based on high fructose corn syrup. If all you considered was the GI, you would say carrots are bad for fat storage, and soft drinks are fine, but of course common sense, nature and, in this case, science must prevail. Enter the GL.

The GL is the GI multiplied by the amount of food you would actually have to eat to ingest the 50 grams of carbohydrate. So with carrots, you would have to eat an entire truck load to go close to eating fifty grams of carbs from carrots. I've not met anyone who has done that, and I'm not suggesting you try! So even though carrots have a high GI, they have a low GL, whereas soft drinks have nothing going for them from a nutritional perspective and have a very high GL, despite having a low GI. Plus we now understand the impact excessive fructose has on the liver. Nature shows us we are supposed to eat our carbs with fiber as this helps make a carb low GL. Nature gets it right. Use common sense. Choose low HI food.

THE NERVOUS SYSTEM

Exercise influences our nervous system as does everything else, including the food we eat and the thoughts we think. Most people believe that in order to become healthy they must lose some weight. I believe the opposite is true; in order to lose weight, we must become healthy, and I approach weight loss in this way. As I've described using science, emotion, and real-life stories throughout this book, I have known thousands of people who subsist off very little, exercise rampantly, but never get anywhere when it comes to fat loss. How else can we approach this? And how does this lifestyle create what I lovingly call the Rushing Woman Syndrome? For some, the RW Syndrome is the heart of them becoming *Accidentally Overweight*. Don't get me wrong. I meet women living the RW Syndrome life, and they are slim. But their nervous systems are usually a wreck.

To understand this, we need to explore how the autonomic nervous system (ANS) works. The autonomic nervous system "runs" our body behind the scenes, and it is not under our conscious control. It regulates our heart rate, our respiration rate, our temperature control, and our immune and hormonal systems while we carry on with life. Don't you think it is truly miraculous that if you cut yourself the wound just heals? Don't you think it is amazing that you swallow food and your digestive system extracts the nutrients to nourish you so you can stay alive? The human body is extraordinary, and that's an understatement.

There are three parts to the autonomic nervous system. They are the sympathetic nervous system (SNS), the parasympathetic nervous system (PNS), and the enteric nervous system (ENS). But I'm going to focus on the sympathetic nervous system, the "fight or flight" system, and the parasympathetic nervous system, the "rest and repair" system, and their interaction.

In general, the SNS and the PNS have opposite functions. When we are under stress, the SNS, as discussed in the stress hormones chapter, raises our heart rate, increases our respiratory rate, releases cortisol, and shunts blood away from the digestive tract to the muscles so that we can run away from or fight whatever is threatening us. If organ systems in the body are unhealthy and therefore stressed themselves, or if we are mentally or emotionally stressed, that increases the sympathetic load as well. The SNS by its very nature is catabolic, meaning that it breaks down muscle tissue due to the increased amounts of secreted cortisol. High-intensity exercise is also sympathetic in nature; the heart rate goes up, as does respiration and body temperature, and cortisol is released into the blood. And we know what cortisol does to body fat and the hormonal changes it initiates. Once the threat is dealt with (is it ever dealt with in the modern world?), the PNS slows our heart rate and respiration, brings the blood back to the digestive tract so that we can digest our food and be well nourished, works on repairing any tissues that have been damaged in our "battle," and allows libido to be restored. Your survival instinct can't have you thinking about sex when your body believes that your life is being threatened! The PNS is able to do its wonderful work overnight, provided we go to bed early enough, because cortisol naturally starts to rise around 2:00 am. The SNS and the PNS are designed to balance each other, and, in those people who have a well-balanced nervous system, high intensity exercise will lead to fat loss because the parasympathic rest time between workouts is when muscle tissue is built.

It is likely that people who are unable to lose fat by doing regular high-intensity exercise have a dominant SNS and, as a result, an inhibited PNS. In situations like this, there is too much systemic stress coming from somewhere, and therefore adding high-intensity exercise is counterproductive, since it adds to an individual's sympathetic load, exacerbating the nervous system imbalance. This is one of the reasons we have to get our heads around "it's not about the calories." If "burning" more of them has not solved your body-fat challenge up until now, it is not suddenly going to start until some other work is done.

Anxiety is so incredibly common today, often as a result of relationship challenges, financial stress, a poor diet and its consequences, or worries about health and weight loss. Yet, a person may be in sympathetic overload and still not even mention feeling anxious.

Reducing the sympathetic load is essential to fat loss if the SNS is dominant. Movement is still important, but it is best approached from a different angle and with a different attitude. Far more effective exercise for SNS-dominant people is what I call the more "yin" (gentle, feminine as opposed to "yang," masculine, go go go) exercise types such as tai chi, qi gong, yoga, or any exercise that is done slowly and while being conscious of the breath. These types of exercise significantly assist in increasing PNS activity, which helps balance the ANS. Once the body is better balanced and healthier, body fat is readily burnt.

I hope that it is quite clear that although this book is about solving your weight loss puzzle, I am also trying to gently unfold information that might open your eyes and your heart to the concept that weight loss involves the superb interaction of many biochemical systems, and that your thoughts, beliefs, and perceptions are just as powerful, if not more powerful than the food you eat.

Lousie Hay teaches that blood glucose is all about the sweetness we perceive in our life. In Type 2 diabetes or insulin resistance, when the blood sugar is elevated, she suggests that your perception of your life is that you have nothing to look forward to. If this resonates for you, I suggest you schedule things in your life that you love and start to notice the immense beauty around you. You can look forward to the surprise of what the sunrise will look like tomorrow.

SOLUTIONS FOR INSULIN

- Eat food the way it comes in nature as often as you can.
    - Limit foods out of packets.
    - Limit refined sugar and foods that have had sugar added to them; after beautiful cane juice is squeezed out of sugar cane, the liquid is processed fourteen times to create the white powder that you then eat. There is zero goodness in sugar.
    - As I said earlier, I live in the same

world as you with the same food on offer, and I want this book to offer practical solutions for you. I encourage you to be strict in the initial phases of change, partly to show you how good you can feel but also to break your habits. If you firstly need to increase your greens before omitting sugar, then do that. And then cut it out for four weeks. No excuses—stevia is a good option for sweetening drinks or cooking.

- Eat carbs only the way they come in nature for four weeks.

  o Eat lentils, berries, and other fruits, but keep fruit to two pieces a day maximum to really get the carbohydrate content of your diet down. Please note, this does not mean cut the carbs out. It means just what I said, which is don't eat carbs out of packets, and limit fruit to two pieces per day.

  o Limit alcohol, as it drives an enormous blood glucose surge and a rapid elevation of insulin.

- If you do drink alcohol, consume it with food.

- Many people are actually hungry and/or thirsty when they want a drink. Do an experiment. If it is the sugar (carbs) in the alcohol you want, eat a carrot or have a sparkling water in a wine glass with some fresh lemon or lime. Notice if the fizz from the water or the coldness of the drink helps quench your thirst.

- Most people tell me that if they make it past the "witching hour" their desire for alcohol passes. Get some strategies to get past this time in your day.

- Have blood tests for blood glucose levels (BGL) and blood insulin.

- Eat five to six small meals per day.
- Eat every three hours.
- Eat protein with every meal.
- Build muscle with resistance training.
  - Chromium and cinnamon can be excellent at supporting healthy blood glucose levels.

  - Insulin is a growth factor and a fat

storage hormone. Skin tags are a sign that there has been a period of time (current or past) where your insulin was likely in excess.

- Cow's milk is made by cows to feed their young. It is created to grow a 90 pound calf into a nearly 2000 pound beast. Humans were never designed to grow at these rates. Limit or omit it, and, if you do consume it, only eat organic dairy.

- Apply the liver and adrenal support strategies.

- Avoid artificial sweeteners as we have no idea of their long-term effect on the human body. I pray they are safe as people consume masses of them these days. There is an enormous difference between exposing mice under test conditions to a substance for less than a year and humans consuming them for their entire lifetime. I am also suspicious that although they do not contain calories, they are confusing the insulin response. Some of the physically largest people I have ever met drank literally liters of diet soft drinks every day, almost like an addiction. Leave it on the shelf. Use sparkling water with fresh fruit to sweeten the transition.

Alkalinity
Puzzle Piece Number 8

The concept of alkalinity can be a confusing one. It relates to the pH of your blood. Everything you eat and drink eventually has an effect on your blood pH. Green vegetables and lemons are almost the only foods that have an alkaline effect on your blood. Alkalinity is vital, not only for burning body fat but for outstanding health, energy, and vitality. Read on!

BONE HEALTH AND ALKALINITY

Bone health is also governed by alkalinity. Your

bones are storage houses of calcium and magnesium, minerals that by their very nature are alkaline. If the blood pH is constantly pushed to be slightly more acidic than is ideal, the blood sends a message to the bones to release calcium and magnesium back out into the blood. As far as the blood is concerned, bones are simply there to provide support for the blood, not for our body structure. Since the blood has to be maintained at all costs, blood health comes first and always takes priority over the bones. When the dietary impact on the blood is too acidic, your bones slowly become thinner due to the constant release of minerals which are attempting to shift the blood pH to be more alkaline.

So even though you might be highly committed to meeting your daily dietary calcium needs, all you may be doing is topping up what you drag out each day, slowly weakening and thinning the bones. I believe that this is a major reason why we see so much osteoporosis in the Western world compared to those consuming what is best described as a "rural Chinese diet." This way of eating is based on plenty of green vegetables, rice, often some fish, and very little else. It is highly alkaline in its ratios due to the high vegetable content. Even breakfast traditionally contains vegetables.

The Western diet is typically low in alkalizing

foods and high in foods that, after digestion, push your blood chemistry to the less alkaline (more acidic) end of its pH spectrum—specifically alcohol, coffee, and processed foods. Red meat also drives acidity in the blood, but if you like red meat and you feel it serves your health, which, for many but not all people, good quality organic cuts can, you can balance the acid push from the meat by having more green vegetables on your plate.

I am not denying the importance of calcium in our diets. It is an essential nutrient that must be consumed daily. In the West, we are told that we need about 1200 milligrams per day, whereas studies from Asia have indicated that the average intake is about 400 milligrams per day. Yet, it is the West experiencing the explosion in osteoporosis. Something to think about.

When it comes to body fat, the best way to imagine how alkalinity plays a role is to imagine how car battery acid might burn your skin if it touches your hand. To exaggerate, when blood is constantly pushed to the acidic end of its spectrum, the cells of your body are bathed in it, so to protect themselves from the acid burn, they insulate themselves with fat.

To make the cells feel safe so that they can let go of their layer of fatty protection, we need to push our chemistry to be more alkaline.

The following is an article I wrote for a January issue of a magazine in the Southern hemisphere that explains the concept of alkalinity further.

Alkalize Your Life: The forgotten factor in fat burning

Imagine a world where burning body fat is as easy as 1, 2, 3. Too good to be true? Perhaps, given the impact poor liver function and stress can have on our waistlines. However, there is a way of eating that can make an enormous difference to whether your body is willing to let go of some unwanted kilos, and there's no better time to change your approach to food and nutrition than in summer, after the seasonal festivities.

The word to keep in the front of your mind is "alkalinity." When our body is in an alkaline state, we happily burn body fat, as one of the reasons we store it is to protect our tissues from damage from acidic conditions. As we know, acid burns, and when your blood and tissues (e.g. your muscles) are too acidic, we tend to hang on to our body fat as a way to protect our blood vessels and vital tissues from damage.

So what is alkalinity and how do we achieve it? Our body is governed by pH ranges, a measure of how acidic or alkaline substances are. Your body works hard to keep all body fluids and tissues at their optimal pH levels, and when these are disrupted, our health can be compromised. Thrush, for example, can be the result of vaginal flora (bacteria) altering due to pH changes in the reproductive system. To truly treat the condition, you need to modify the pH that led to the condition (and usually treat estrogen dominance) rather than simply treat the symptoms. Otherwise, the condition returns.

When it comes to body fat loss, it is the pH of our blood that can make such an enormous difference. Your body likes to keep blood pH right in the middle of the normal range. After we digest our food, the end result will either push the pH of our blood to be more acidic or alkaline. Blood is always slightly alkaline but the lower the pH inside this alkaline range, the more acidic it is considered to be.

Vegetables are virtually the only food to push our blood to the alkaline end of the scale, which is why I am very happy to say that most people can safely double the amount of green vegetables they usually eat. Not that most people want to hear this! Almost all other foods push our blood to be more acidic, although to varying degrees. Therefore, including green foods with most of our meals (or even drinking green snacks) can make an enormous difference to our capacity to burn body fat.

In practical terms, this might mean

juicing a big bunch of green leaves for your breakfast. Try spinach, silver beet, celery, parsley, carrot, and lemon. If initially this is too tart for your taste buds, add the juice of half an apple or some pineapple, then add less of the fruit as you get used to the taste of the greens. After a while, your energy levels will soar! Choose salad or eat left-overs (containing some greens of course!) for lunch five days out of seven. Many of us rely too much on bread at lunchtime at the expense of our greens. Dinner might be your opportunity to steam, blanch or stir-fry some vegetables or to enjoy a big bowl of salad, keeping in mind that any left-overs will be handy for lunch the next day. Vegetables that have been well cooked in a casserole for example, still have alka-line properties so are also wonderful to include.

I can't encourage you enough to increase your consumption of green foods, but if you're giggling at the thought of hav-ing enough time to make a vegetable juice in the morning, then try one of the many "green drinks" available, such as barley grass, wheat grass, or spirulina. You can buy these as powders or capsules, and they can be a great addition to your diet, especially when travelling.

It is a complex concept, but all you need to keep in mind is that alkalinity promotes body fat loss, good bone health, energy, and vitality, and, to achieve this state, base your diet on green foods. Cover your plate in them as often as you can, and then add concentrated food to that, such as protein and/or carbohydrates.

Investing in alkalinity also means that some of our other acid-promoting ways have a significantly reduced impact on our health. So perhaps burning body fat is as easy as ABC rather than 1, 2, 3! And of course A stands for alkaline!

FOOD COMBINING

Food combining is a wonderful approach to eating that can enhance digestion, energy, vitality, and fat loss, and it can be a great way to combat a bloated tummy. It involves never eating animal protein with any form of carbohydrates. In practice, that means no meat with potatoes. It means that if you eat meat, chicken, or fish, you need to eat it with vegetables that have a high water content, not starchy ones, such as potato, sweet potato (kumera), pumpkin, corn, or any other starchy foods such as pasta, bread, or rice.

If you eat vegetable protein, such as one of the many types of lentils, chickpeas, beans, or tempeh, then, under food combining principles, you do not eat meat with these foods, but rather any vegetable at all, including starchy ones if they appeal. If you feel like eating rice, then, with food combining, it needs to be a vegetarian meal. Seeds and nuts are also best eaten with vegetarian meals and not with meals containing animal protein due to the vegetable protein content of the nuts and seeds. Oils and other foods rich in fats including avocado can be eaten with either animal-based meals or starch-based meals.

Another principle of food combining is that fruit can only be consumed as your first meal and not again during the day. You are also encouraged to omit all refined sugar due to its acidifying effects on the blood. I know people who live by the concept of food combining and feel spectacular. If you want to try it, but it seems a little extreme, apply the zigzag principle. This means that most of the time you follow food-combining practices (zig), but one day a week—or two to three meals a week if you'd prefer (I suggest one day... or one meal!)—you relax and zag. This way, food combining becomes a sustainable way to live as you are able to socialize without feeling restricted and you can also eat the foods you love, just not every day. It is a structured way of eating on which some people literally thrive, and I have seen it truly change people's lives. For others, though, food combining would take every aspect of joy out

of their lives. If you feel like this is not for you. Use
the zigzag concept if you do want to use food combining, or apply other strategies in this book.

THE DIFFERENCE BETWEEN DIGESTION ACIDITY
AND BLOOD ALKALINITY

It can be confusing when you hear about the
importance of acidity in the digestive system and
the importance of alkalinity in the blood. When it is
said like this, it is clear they are two distinct systems.
As discussed in the digestion section, having optimal
acid levels in the stomach is essential for effective
digestion, both in the stomach itself, plus to set up
the pH gradient as the digestive tract continues. As
discussed earlier, if the acid in the stomach is not
acidic enough, the food will not be broken down
correctly, and partially undigested food will end up
too far along the digestive tract. If this occurs, the
food ferments, and this drives undesirable gut bacteria to take up residence in the colon. These bacteria
often make lactic acid, which further impairs digestion and nutrient absorption, not to mention liver
function. Poor digestion has an acidifying effect on
blood chemistry.

Blood chemistry is a completely separate system,
and the digestive system is just one of the things that
can affect blood pH. As I've explained, blood pH is

always alkaline. Optimal health occurs with a blood pH of around 7.4, right in the middle of the normal range, which is usually considered to be 7.35 to 7.45. Any pH below 7.4 is the "acidic" end of that range and is not desirable.

SOLUTIONS TOWARD MORE ALKALINE BLOOD

- Buy a juicer and juice vegetables each morning.

- Make a green smoothie by blending a banana, a pear and a bunch of spinach with some water in a blender. That way you get all of the goodness from the fruits and vegetables. Nothing is discarded. A great start to the day.

- Take a green drink supplement.

- Optimize digestion by applying the solutions offered in the Digestion section.

- Cover your plate with green vegetables for a minimum of two meals a day, five days a week; make them tasty by using herbs (also usually green), and cook and serve them differently each day. Plus, use different vegetables from day to day. There are so many vegetables in nature, but we tend to stick to the same ones each day. At least you are eating them, though!

- Breathe using your diaphragm for twenty long, slow breaths five (preferably seven) days a week.

- If you eat animal protein, eat it separately from starch.

- Eat fruit on an empty stomach, and only first thing in the morning, not as a snack.

Emotions
Puzzle Piece Number 9

Most of us know what to eat, we just don't do it. Even with the confusing nutrition information out there such as "eat carbs as they are essential for energy" versus "don't eat carbs because they make you fat and tired" (and these statements can be made in books sitting right beside one another on the same book shelf!); most of us still have a general idea about the food that nourishes us. And we still don't do it. And this is not just about food and body size. I've met plenty of slim people who are incredibly unhealthy. Just because it might not show on the outside doesn't mean you've got this piece of the puzzle licked. Most of us know it is not great to drink bucket loads of alcohol or caffeine either, yet at times we still do.

If food, certain beverages, your body, or your weight are areas with which you struggle and argue about in your mind, you can spend your life in search of the right diet or the magic bullet or a time in your life when you are not so stressed and will finally be able to focus on your health. These things never come of their own accord. We always plan to do it tomorrow.

Since you already know how to eat and drink, my words are simply to remind you of what you already know. Some of you may not actually want to hear it even though you tell yourself you'd do anything for better health, a slimmer body, or both. Nature gets it right when it comes to food. So mostly choose these foods. Sure, there can be areas with which you need some guidance for a specific health picture, such as estrogen dominance, anxiety, or insulin resistance. And that is certainly what health professionals are for. And if you are confused about what to eat, then we guide you with that, too. In fact, I always guide people with the practicalities of solving estrogen dominance, anxiety, or insulin resistance (for example), so the results begin to be obtained and also because these changes can be a stepping stone to the emotions we actually need to explore.

Some emotions don't surface until you start going without what has been your numbing device: food, coffee, or alcohol. What I am saying is that if you are physically too big for optimal health, then it is usually not a lack of knowledge that got you there. If it were as simple as applying what you know, then you would have lost weight years ago. In fact, you would never have put it on in the first place. So the questions is, why don't you eat in a way that makes you look and feel your best? Why? And, as I said, this is not just about body size. It can be just as much about body symptoms such as reflux, sinus congestion, or diarrhea. If you eat or drink something, while in your heart you know it gives you reflux, blocked sinuses, or loose stools, what are you communicating to your body? You're saying, "I'm not listening."

Why do we do it? In my opinion, there will be a range of reasons, but they virtually all lead back to the same statement you are unconsciously telling yourself: "I don't really care about you."

The first way to begin to explore an emotional approach to eating is to go digging for what food means to you. The second way is about cognitively understanding your emotional landscape and the meanings and rules that you touch on regularly that fuel your life. The third is through the examination and the application of the principles and processes of your Em-Matrix ("Em" stands for emotional)— your emotional patterns. There is so much gold right here.

FOOD IS...

As I outlined in the Calories piece of the puzzle, one of the first exercises I do with my clients when they want to get to the heart of why they overeat (or over-consume alcohol, although we will focus on food here), is to ask them to complete the following sentence with the first word that flies into their head, no censorship.

I say, "Food is..." and they respond: "Yummy," "delicious," "a pain in the neck," "life," "love," "my whole world," "comfort," "amazing." These are all words that quickly and easily fly out of people's mouths. For someone who has gained and lost the same 40 to 100 pounds over the years, food frequently falls into the "pleasure" category. If I am going to guide someone to change the way they eat, and food is their biggest source of pleasure in life, if I don't delve into what else this person finds pleasurable and point this out and encourage them to experience more of this in their lives (such as connecting with the beauty of nature, their faith, or how playful their puppy is), the food changes will be temporary. Food either needs a new meaning, such as nourishment, or energy, or the other pleasure factors need amped up in this person's life. Even just being aware of what food means to you is a great first step.

One of my favorite examples to share about how this simple process changed a client's after dinner food frenzy comes from a precious lady for whom food was mostly comfort. Julie had experienced huge emotional trauma, and, afterward, food had become her friend, her sweetness, and her joy in life. When she came to see me, she said she was so desperate to lose the weight, she believed it had affected her work, as her job was in the public spotlight and she was embarrassed by her growing size. When I did the "Food is…" exercise with her, it become clear that what she wanted was comfort.

I asked her how else she might find comfort in a way that did not involve food. I'd listened as we'd been speaking about how much she treasured her precious daughters, and from her descriptions they sounded very sweet. I felt that when she ate in the evenings what she really wanted was a hug, to be comforted emotionally by another human, or by something bigger (in a spiritual sense), rather than by food. I asked her if she ever stood at the door of her girls' bedrooms and watched them sleeping. Tears immediately sprang to Julie's eyes. As Mark Twain said, "Any emotion if it is sincere, is involuntary," so I immediately knew this was meaningful to her. I suggested that, each evening after the girls had gone to bed, Julie complete her usual evening rituals in the kitchen and, instead of going straight to the fridge and into the lounge room for a private sweet feast and the TV, she go to her girls and watch them sleeping. I suggested she notice their breaths, the little lights in their rooms, their innocence, the delicate smell of their hair, and the way their arms poked out from beneath the covers. I invited her to take comfort from their presence in her life. I reminded her that she created them and that, for now, if the only way I could get her to appreciate how truly amazing she was, was by focusing on the little girls she had brought into this world, then that would be the best "medicine" in the world for her. We both cried, and Julie knew with conviction that she had her perfect answer. After just four weeks of practice, her weight had fallen, and she had not even heard the call of sweet food. She had sweetness in spades watching her children sleep.

Another point worthy of mention is that of food waste. So many people eat too much food because they don't want to waste it, a behavior that is often derived from childhood experiences. A client once told me that she had chickens in her backyard so she could give all of her leftovers to them. That was how she "managed" her challenge with throwing food out. For some, it simply takes a change of perception: Whether you throw it out or you overeat, either way it is a waste.

UNDERSTAND YOUR MEANINGS AND RULES: THE FUEL FOR YOUR LIFE

Humans store fat when they do not feel safe, whatever that means to them. I don't necessarily mean safe from burglary, but rather psychologically safe. On a physical level, I can relate such fat storage back to cortisol and the many downstream effects of this catabolic, metabolism-slowing hormone. Yet to truly crack that cortisol challenge, emotions hold the key.

Each of us have rules about what it means for us to feel safe—typically in the areas of relationships, finance, and work—as a result of the life experiences we have had to date. Trouble is, we don't usually know what these rules are. The life experiences to which I am referring don't have to be traumatic. Not in the slightest. What I am referring to are all of the experiences of your life, traumatic or not, that have shaped your personality, your bank balance, your relationships, your responses, and your body size, to name but a few.

Everyone creates explanations about what things mean based on their own experiences in life so far. They are created from the interactions we had as children with the adults around us. As adults, we continue to replay these same meanings, only we are not aware we are doing it. All we know is that we seem to react to people and what they say, or they seem to always react to us in what seems like an inappropriate way, or we forever find ourselves in conflict with certain people. It's like an itch that constantly gets scratched. You are often unaware that this is what's behind so much struggle or suffering in your life (and also the good stuff when the meanings serve you), including your relationship with food, your body, with alcohol, or with your partner. There are some meanings that serve us and some that no longer do. Some are simply outdated protection mechanisms that were set up because of experiences earlier in your life. And where once they might have kept you safe, now they simply hold you back.

The meanings and rules to which I am referring were (and still are being) written by your unconscious mind, the part of your mind that makes your heart beat and your hair grow without you having to tell them to do so. This part of your mind processes two to four million pieces of information per second, while your conscious mind only processes around 134 pieces of information per second. Think about that. I mean, *really* think about that. Your unconscious is extremely powerful.

SPECIFIC MEANINGS AND RULES

The psychology of eating is a fascinating area. In every person, there are emotions that, although we don't realize it, are incredibly painful for us to feel. These are typically rejection, failure, and guilt. There are many more, but for the simplicity's sake I will keep it to these three. All three may be a factor for someone, but there is almost always one stand out… many women, for example, are what I endearingly call "love bugs." Although men also find rejection painful, as adults the fear of feeling this emotion is often buried under another emotion they fear such as failure. Ouch!

A love bug functions between two polarities every day: love and rejection. Replace the word "love" with "connection" or "appreciation" if that helps you relate to this idea, but I'll keep using "love" to keep it simple. Without realizing it, we behave as if we want a life jam-packed with love—caring for others and ourselves, feeling appreciated and understood, living without conflict, the list is almost endless. Yet psychology 101 teaches us that humans will do more to avoid pain than they will ever do to have pleasure. So instead of behaving in a way that drives a life of love, we spend our lives trying to avoid rejection… and those two lives look very different.

Based on our life experiences, we have rules in our unconscious minds about what has to happen for us to feel love and rules about what has to happen for us to feel rejected. Most of us make it really easy for ourselves to feel the emotion we actually want to avoid, which, in this case, is rejection. Simultaneously, our rules around love make it really hard for us to feel it easily or constantly. An example that has brought tears to countless women's eyes as they have shared it with me during a session is this one.

You drop your son at the school gate and catch the eye of another mom you have previously noticed and admired. For the first time, you have a lovely chat and although there may be no conscious thought about this event lifting your spirits, you carry on happily with your day. But that afternoon, when you collect your son from school, your new acquaintance snubs you. She looks straight through you. You wonder what you've done wrong. Did you offend her? Did you embarrass yourself? Did you mistake her interest in you when really she just had no one better to talk to? Did she only speak to you because not many other moms were around that morning? So many questions! Isn't it exhausting what we put ourselves through?

What you probably actually touch on in this moment is an inkling that you are not good enough. And for the millionth time in your life, you scratch this itch. Unfortunately, you don't realize that this is what you're doing—and what you have probably done many times in the past. All you know is that now you feel sad or irritated. You may start focusing on how big your thighs look in your jeans or listening to other negative self-talk. You might decide you want some wine or some food that doesn't really benefit you. As soon as you have even had this thought, you feel a little bit better because now you have something to look forward to.

Again, it's unlikely that you will consciously make the connection between your new acquaintance, your "I'm not good enough" button, and your mood, but rather than skipping through your afternoon, you feel flat and frustrated. Or perhaps you are simply in a bad mood, despite looking forward to your cake, your crackers, or your wine (or the whole shebang!), when your morning had been rather delightful or at least not emotionally eventful. Who is usually on the receiving end of your sullen or irritated mood? Most often, you direct it toward yourself and also the people you love the most in this world. Of course it's obvious, you tell yourself, that your new acquaintance is too embarrassed to speak to you when certain other mothers are around because you're a bit fat. So, just to prove to yourself that you really aren't good enough, you eat. Without realizing it, you want to prove yourself right; that you are, indeed, useless and have no willpower. No wonder you are fat; that must be why people don't like you and your mother told you that you were an embarrassment. And it was actually way back then, starting with some comment your mother made, when you first felt "not good enough." Not that she meant to hurt your feelings and not that you can see any of this when you are in the throes of inhaling a box of crackers, half a block of cheese, and a few glasses of white wine...

As for your family, or whoever else is on the receiving end of your change in mood, they don't understand why you are overreacting to things that didn't bother you yesterday, or what they seem to have done wrong. Of course they haven't done anything. Through food and/or wine, you have simply escaped from the "pain," from the deep, human, primal fear that you are not good enough and therefore you won't be loved. The bottom line is you feel rejected by your new acquaintance.

What if I told you that she didn't see you or she didn't register seeing you? You will tell me that you *saw* her see you. I will tell you to ask yourself a life-changing question... "I wonder what might be going on for her?" How do you know what it is like to be her? How do you know that she doesn't have a million things to do before she gets home, where she has to make sure the house is perfect and the children are bathed and fed so that when her husband arrives home he won't raise his voice and tell her that she is useless and does nothing all day? What if that is *her* ultimate pain because her mother or father told her the same thing?

What if I told you that her perceived "snub" of you had nothing to do with you and that, whatever her story, her "snub" speaks volumes about her? Love bugs need to ask "I wonder what might be going on for them quite regularly, until they can stop the daggers of "rejection" from penetrating their hearts. I had a client for whom this question changed not just her life but her body, and I will never forget the glee on her face when she told me it had freed her from what she called "agony," which involved secret eating after dinner and awful self-talk as a consequence. She literally looked as though years had come off her face just from this new understanding.

If love bugs find themselves standing at the fridge, peering in as if the meaning of life must be contained inside, another useful question to ask yourself is, "What do I really want?" At first, your brain will probably tell you that of course you simply want the chocolate or the box of cookies, but if you keep asking yourself this question the veil will start to lift, and you will see that what you actually want is a hug or company or to feel appreciated. And that's when you absolutely must give *yourself* exactly what you want. Find ways to give yourself the gifts you desire.

EMOTIONAL PAIN CAN SERVE YOU

The belief that to feel emotional pain is too traumatic to bear is like looking at the world through the eyes of a child. As infants, if we didn't have love, attention, and someone to feed us, we would die. So when we are born, a powerful belief is born as well: without love, we will die. The thing is, of course, while a child might perish without love, adults physically will not. Love is delicious yes, but we won't die without it. The trouble is, if you "touch" this belief too easily because your unconscious mind is set up, then your desire to escape from emotions you won't let yourself feel, let alone recognize, can be a constant and overwhelming battle. To escape, some people choose food; some people drink two bottles of wine every night. Some people chain-smoke a pack of cigarettes each day. Some exercise like they are possessed. Some people talk incessantly, some people eat. And every time you do this, you miss out on feeling what is really there. It is the desire to avoid this "pain," that makes you bolt. You bolt to the fridge, and you bolt from yourself and what you truly feel in that moment. Your way back home to yourself—and away from the fridge or whatever escape mechanism you use—lies in acknowledging the pain and truly experiencing that it will not kill you. If you feel sad, you feel sad. If you overeat regularly to blanket the sadness, you just give yourself an additional reason to be sad. Eating does not get rid of the sadness. It adds to it. Why not then simply acknowledge that you feel sad rather than escaping from your pain through food?

Let's break this down into a strategy you can work on. The first step is to recognize an emotion that is very tough for you to feel, whether it's rejection, failure, or guilt, and then explore what has to happen for you to feel this emotion. You will see that humans make it really easy to feel emotions that we perceive will bring us the most pain and that we therefore most want to avoid. Unless you have previously done some work in this area, the emotion you first want to work with was (more than likely) created from an experience you had when you were probably quite young.

I'll give you another simple example to get you thinking. One of the first people I ever did this work with was a publicly well-known woman who was "larger than life" (I'll call her Mary). Mary was gregarious, hilarious, likeable, financially successful and, as a result, very charitable. She arrived to see me with a statement that went something like "I've heard you do weight loss differently and, honey, I've tried everything." Mary went on to tell me that she felt "successful" in every area of her life except when it came to her body. She never mentioned "health." In everything she said, it was always about her size and weight; until I asked, she never mentioned her reflux, the trouble she had breathing, the regular headaches, or the eczema that had been present since childhood. "Health" was not on her radar. It's very useful to start noticing your language patterns because a great deal can be revealed through what you say and also what you don't say. The other thing I noticed was the way she spoke about her mother. She hadn't just been irritated by her mother; she despised her. She spoke about her in the present tense, so I was stunned to learn that her mother had actually passed away almost twenty years before. When I asked Mary if there was a time in her life when she could recall her relationship with her mother not being so diabolical, she said yes. I knew "something" had happened and that was the place, in her case, we needed to begin. There is so much gold in the "why."

Mary thought the direction I was taking our session was a "load of rubbish," particularly as she'd already done years of therapy around her hatred for her mother. She paid lip service to the concept that her mother had done her best, but when she finished that statement with "blah, blah, blah," a roll of her eyes, and a wave of her hand, I knew her heart didn't believe it. So I dived deeper. After all, she'd ask me to help her be as "successful" with her weight as she was in other areas of her life.

I asked Mary to remember a time when things were dreadful between her and her mother and then also a time when it had felt fine, or even quite good, to be around her mother. She said she could remember both. Then I asked her to remember the day it changed. And for the first time, her face lost its intensity and tightness. When Mary was four years old, she had been playing outside by herself, not far from the house on the family farm. She fell and cut her eye, screaming as she did so. Her mother came running from the house and shouted, "You should be more careful, and then you wouldn't get hurt."

In that moment, my client could have created any of the following meanings:

- My mother thinks I'm a failure (failure).

- My mother hates me and doesn't love me (rejection).

- I've disappointed my mother (guilt).

- My mother loves me so much she wants to protect me from further injury/pain (love).

- Hooray! I got Mum's attention (success).

Before we move on, contemplate why you think the mother responded this way. Could her thoughts have been:

- My precious baby has fallen and hurt herself for the first time! I must warn her to be more careful so she doesn't get hurt again (love).

- I feel so guilty that I wasn't there to protect my baby girl (her own guilt).

- I am so useless because my baby has hurt herself (failure).

You can see from the outside that the mother's response to her child's accident came from a place of love and protection. But for Mary it was the first time her mother raised her voice at her and she had now linked it to physical pain. Welcome to a new "meaning" locked into your nervous system. This is how the "itch" I describe gets set up for constant scratching as you go through life.

The mother's delivery may have been rough or harsh, but the intention was beautiful. Yet when I asked Mary what she thought her mother meant from the words she had spoken, she told me she was a "cruel, cruel woman who hated me." In that moment, when she was four, Mary created a meaning that her mother didn't love her. In her eyes, "how could anyone who loves you shout at you when you're hurt?" *(Please note, these words are not intended to illicit any feelings of guilt for parents. Please keep in mind that creating meanings from what others say is part of being human (every one does it) and yes it shapes us and who we become but it gives us the opportunity to learn and grow and contribute. The skill comes with being able to step back and see the "story" you are telling yourself).*

That moment set up further challenging interactions between Mary and her mother. Why? Because, remember, once you have a belief, whether you recognize it or not, you set about proving yourself right, so you look for evidence of what you believe anywhere and everywhere. So, for example, when you are seven years old and you are leaving the house for school, and your mother calls out, possibly again in a frustrated voice because she has 80000 things to do that day and is running late, "It's cold outside and you've forgotten your jumper. Go and get your jumper." If you were Mary in the situation, and had, in that first instance when you fell, created a meaning of "wow, my mom loves me so much she never wants me to go through this pain again" (love), then when your mother tells you to get your jumper, you would have skipped off to your room, grabbed your jumper, and happily gone off to school, regardless of the tone in her voice. In fact, you probably wouldn't even have noticed her "tone." If, however, from that first instance, you created a meaning of rejection or failure, you would hear that meaning in your mother's words reminding you to take your jumper to school, and you would validate that meaning by saying to yourself, "See, she doesn't even think I can dress myself." You will stomp off to your room, collect your jumper, and go sullenly to school, only to have your mood lighten once you arrive and see your friends.

Can you see how two completely different lives could play out just from that one meaning that was created so early?

When you are little, from a psychological development perspective, you are the center of the universe. It is all about you. It has to be or you wouldn't survive, remember. But once you are older and have the opportunity to see such situations as if you are hovering above them, that clarity can be enough to illicit the most beautiful "healing," the most magnificent "a-ha" moments. When an adult "sees" a mistaken belief from childhood, the forgiveness and compassion for their parent's life is palpable and always an honor to witness.

It is important to witness that the meanings we've created for ourselves have served us until now. Indeed they may not have always brought you challenges. Until now, some of the meanings you have created will have done some great things for you. For example, if you were a part of the scenario above and the initial meaning you created was guilt, then you may have spent your life pleasing everyone so you never felt like you were letting anyone down and so people probably love and appreciate you. For Mary, on the other hand, feeling rejected with a decent amount of "I'm a failure" thrown in, caused her to develop an "I'll show you" attitude, meaning she was determined to create an extraordinary life to show her mother that she was successful and therefore loveable. This not only influenced the development of her likeable personality, but also made her financially successful, enabling her to give back to charities in enormous ways. So her meanings fostered a lot of good.

But there often comes a point when the meanings we've created may no longer serve us. For example, if you are always pleasing people to stop them from feeling disappointed in you so you can avoid guilt, it is likely to become exhausting after a while, and could deplete your adrenal glands, which may be the basis of your health problems. For Mary, she ate huge volumes of food most nights as a way of avoiding the reality that all she ever really wanted was her mother's love. She would never have seen that because the hatred she'd constructed was so vast. When Mary could see that her mother had actually always loved her, her fat literally began to fall away.

Sometimes all it takes is a glimpse of the "truth" for a shift to occur, leading to an effortless change in food behavior and a glorious letting go of the blanket of protection (body fat) that may have been carried for decades. For others, I take them through a process that I first learned at an amazing event conducted by Tony Robbins, called Date With Destiny. I recognize the significant contribution Tony has made to this world by deciphering so much of human psychology, and I am very grateful to him for his insights and strategies.

WHAT ARE YOUR RULES?

The process I take my clients through involves

first recognizing and writing down what currently has to happen for them to feel love. Then I ask them to write down what currently has to happen for them to feel rejected. We review the answers together and usually giggle or cry our way through them as they begin to see the conflicts. Some examples are below.

Question: What emotion do you want to feel regularly?

Answer: Love

Write down what *currently* has to happen for you to feel love?

- He has to look at me with soft, gentle eyes, smile like he really means it, and reach out and touch my hand all at the same time.

- He can *never* raise his voice at me.

- He can *never* use anything but a nice tone with me.

- He can *never* be late.

- He can *never* play computer games when there are jobs to do around the house.

- He *always* has to notice when I am over-whelmed and help me, even if I haven't asked.

- *No one* can *ever* ignore me!

- He *always has to* know when I'm too tired

for sex and leave me alone and not make me feel guilty.

Doing this exercise is usually the first time someone realizes how tough they make it on themselves to feel and experience a given emotion, in this case love. Notice the language... it is absolute, featuring words such as "never" and "always." Additionally, most people have no idea that this is what they really want, so how on earth is their partner supposed to? No wonder this particular lady was so angry with her husband. She never felt like he loved her because he didn't do all of the above! Besides, how do you explain to someone that they "can *never* use anything but a nice tone" with you?!? We are very funny, we humans.

The next step is to do the current rejection list.

Question: What emotion is really painful for you to feel?

Answer: Rejection

Write down what *currently* has to happen for you to feel rejected?

- If he raises his voice at me.

- If he doesn't look me in the eye.

- If a colleague, who usually stops by to say hi when he walks past my office, doesn't.

- If someone ignores me.

- If someone doesn't hear me.

- If someone questions my work and asks me why I've done what I've done.

A "rejection" story that exemplifies what I mean involves a client and one of her colleagues. My client didn't enjoy her job, so the highlight of her day was her colleague stopping by her office to chat on his way back from the coffee machine. They mostly chatted about things other than work and he stopped by every day. Until he didn't! One day, he walked past (she said marched past) and didn't stop to chat. In that moment, virtually every female on the planet would be like my client and ask herself "What have I done?" It can take us two minutes, two days, two weeks, or two years before we pause to think "I wonder what might be going on for him." By then, you have tortured yourself with every possible scenario of how you could have offended him, even though you've done nothing at all. Perhaps he just had piles of work to get through and he forgot to stop. Maybe he had a sick child and was racing back to his desk in case the phone rang. I could hypothesize for hours. My points is, save yourself a whole lot of heartache, rejection, exhaustion, distraction, and "unresourceful" eating or excessive drinking, and ask yourself, "I wonder what might be going on for him (or her)." He might appreciate your concern. And on the off chance he is upset with you, you can sort it out immediately.

You can see that the items on the list of rejection scenarios above could easily happen fifty times a day. How many times do you think this particular woman experienced "rejection" in a day compared to "love" based on these two sets of "rules"? Even though you don't walk around all day saying, "I feel rejected, I feel rejected, I feel rejected," you might still feel flat, lousy, depressed, angry, irritated, and frustrated. You may loathe yourself because you have scratched your "rejection" itch fifty times that day, and your perception is that you touched on love only twice.

Let me remind you again, *none* of this is conscious. *None* of these thoughts are cognitive in nature. They reveal themselves in your body as a momentary sick feeling in your tummy or a momentary spasm in your back, for example. In that moment, if you wanted to, you could access your sense of rejection. But you've conditioned your conscious mind to never go there (unless it is glaringly obvious). How often you unconsciously "feel" rejection and how often you unconsciously "feel" love is the fuel for your life. Your fuel, your juice, your passion won't show up if you are spending most of your day touching on rejection and feeling lousy. And it is at the end of a day like this, that, if food is your "comfort," your "drug," the way you "bolt," then no amount of "willpower" will ever be able to override your unconscious desperation to avoid actually *feeling* the rejection that, when you were a small child, your conscious mind perceived but decided was just too painful to feel.

There are numerous ways to get out of dodge, to alter the above scenario. The first involves rewriting your rules about what has to happen for you to feel love and rejection and, with practice, your emotional landscape will begin to change. After all, the first set of rules went in without you being conscious of it. Now it's time to direct your own rules! But it's essential to practice your new rules once you have them. Another modality I want to share with you is called Network Spinal Analysis (NSA), a powerful, non-cracking form of chiropractic that also encompasses a particular type of breathing called Somato (body) Respiratory Integration (SRI). It is truly a phenomenal practice. A third way to alter your unconscious responses is to apply a revolutionary, spectacular, and gentle process called the Emotional Matrix ("Em-Matrix"), which we will explore later in this chapter.

Approach rewriting the rules for any of your emotions playfully. The whole idea is to make love, in this case, or success, for example, *really* easy to feel, and, with the new rules we write, to make it really difficult to feel rejection.

Write new rules for yourself about how you will feel your desired, or what we'll call your "toward" emotion, for example love. Make it *really* easy to feel! Keep the toward emotion in *your* control, not reliant on anyone else.

Start the spiel with "Anytime I ..." and write "or" in between each rule.

For example, "Anytime I ..."

- Smile *or*

- Appreciate nature *or*

- Eat food that nourishes me *or*

- Drink a glass of water *or*

- Hear a bird song *or*

- Exercise *or*

- Write in my diary *or*

- Read a magazine *or*

- Light a candle *or*

- Have a bath *or*

- Etc. ...

You must read these out loud every day for a month and move your body as you say them. You *might* sway gently, dance, walk briskly, or use powerful arm actions. Pay attention when you smile and, after a while, notice a different level of happiness start to emerge from a feeling inside. You will hear more birdsong. You will drink more water, and each time you will not just be listening and appreciating and quenching your thirst, but your nervous system will start to feel "love" from the activities you do that demonstrate love toward yourself.

Now write a new rule for yourself about how you will feel your "away from" emotion, for example rejection. Make it really hard to feel! Make it about you rather than anyone else. Start with "Only if I were to consistently indulge in the debilitating, unresourceful emotion of (for example) rejection, instead of remembering that..."

- ... only I determine how I feel and respond to others, and I have not walked in anyone else's shoes.

It is so important to read your new rules aloud and combine them with body actions. This helps engage your nervous system, allowing your subconscious to be reeducated with rules and meanings that will serve you and allow you to feel and acknowledge how truly amazing you are. Again, I acknowledge

Tony Robbins for this remarkable process.

NETWORK SPINAL ANALYSIS AND SOMATO RESPIRATORY INTEGRATION

There is a school of thought that every cell of our body has a memory for what it (you) has been through. You may have noticed a person's posture perhaps, and used language to describe them (for example) "having the weight of the world on their shoulders". Often, based on their perception of their own life, they will indeed feel this way. An NSA practitioner believes that, via your nervous system, your body stores experiences, both physical and emotional and that our postures, even subtle ones, hold us in these patterns of belief. And when you think about your spine being the "connector" between your brain and your organs, you begin to get an idea of why our spine's health is worth optimizing... for it offers you a gateway between your body and your mind.

Developed by an incredibly gifted man, Donny Epstein, NSA involves gentle, precise touch to the spine which cues the brain to create new wellness strategies. Through working on the physical structure of the body, behavioral change unfolds effortlessly. Through SRI, people are educated to the body's rhythms and their own inner wisdom through focused attention, gentle breath, movement and touch. A big part of SRI behind the scenes is helping the nervous system feel "safe", a place from which new perceptions, healing and optimal health can transform. I personally love these approaches to health and recommend them to everyone and they really need to be experienced to be "understood".

THE EM-MATRIX

What if I told you that every single emotion is here to serve you? What if I told you that every emotion has a gift for you? What if I told you that every emotion has a message for you and that once you hear it, a space will remain for your truth, your core essence to expand into? And what if I told you that instead of delving back into your past to help you cognitively understand why you eat "unresource-fully," we could instead simply and gently explore the emotions and the patterns that exist today. Welcome to the Em-Matrix, a concept and a process the world so desperately needs. Open your mind to this.

An incredibly gifted and generous woman called Deborah Battersby is the founder of a concept called Em-Matrix. Having studied with Deb and her co-founder Dr. Sam Hazeldine, I've discovered how powerful their work is in the way it allows people to gently see how every emotion that we may perceive to be negative, has actually come to serve us.

Deb has created a process that you can be guided through (or with a little experience, you can take yourself through) and that will allow what I've been referring to as your unconscious mind to communicate the real reason a particular pattern or emotion keeps showing up in your life. For example, you really want to quit your job and start your own business, but, every time you come close, you feel frightened. Now fear can serve or fear can hold you back. Guided by the fundamental principle of Em –Matrix that all emotion is here to serve, the gentle and effortless Em-Matrix process allows the "fear" to speak and communicate its wonderful intentions, which could include "to keep you safe" and "offer wisdom." Yet fear may be holding you back from a life that somewhere in your heart could be enormously fulfilling. And when humans aren't fulfilled, many people eat. What I have now seen time and time again is that, once you see that fear was there to help you and it had simply overstayed its welcome, you let it go and you allow your truth to fill the space where once the fear was.

The Em-Matrix process allows your unconscious to "speak" and as a result I've seen very anxious people go from being wired to being centered and stay that way. This process changes your whole nervous system because your old, unconscious thoughts and feelings that once silently wired and unwittingly consumed you now give you strength, passion, and insight.

A simple explanation of how this happens is that when you have a perception that an emotion you feel is negative, your autonomic nervous system activates. It does this because, in that moment, you judge yourself. And if you continue to touch on this emotion frequently and subsequently have too much time in your sympathetic nervous system it will become dominant, bringing with it all of the consequences of too much cortisol. If this pattern or this emotion on some level stops you from truly resting, your parasympathetic nervous system is unable to do the rest and repair work it needs to.

Because your sympathetic nervous system remains dominant, your fight or flight response will be triggered. When it comes to emotions, it's the emotions that we literally "stuff" inside ourselves that drive us to indulge in addictions to keep us distracted from the pain. That's the flight. That's the bolting and the getting out of dodge. The never wanting to return "home" because it is too painful and, gosh, also because that big scary piece of pain that I was so clever to stuff back down inside myself with the cake I ate after dinner might bubble to the surface. So I'll just keep bolting. The fight, on the other hand, is either "suppressed" or it "explodes" in angry outbursts or rage, and the consequences of that not only affect the individual exploding but usually the people around them, too. Whatever you then say to yourself is powerful and keeps your sympathetic nervous system dominant with everything that involves.

I encourage you all to take part in an Em-Matrix Experience. It is such a spectacular yet gentle way to change the patterns and emotional landscape of your life. The distinctions, transformations, and breakthroughs it offers have the potential to change that landscape—to change the world really. Imagine how much less cortisol we would all make! Your thoughts and beliefs are just as powerful, if not more powerful, than anything you put in your mouth.

THE WRAP UP

After all of this talk about food, hormones, alcohol, coffee, and body size, I want to remind you that it is never about the food. Nor is it about the hormones, and yet, at the same time, it is about them because you will feel so much better if you address, for example, your estrogen dominance or insulin resistance. But hear this, please hear this... you would never want the rubbish or the harmful amounts you swallow if you knew who you really were, if you truly had a deep appreciation of how magnificent you are or saw the light that shines inside you, regardless of how dim you tell yourself you are or how dim you think you need to be to fit in. And when you effortlessly decide you don't want the crap, rather than you going without the crap because someone told you to, everything changes, including the estrogen dominance, the insulin resistance, and the body fat you no longer need. You feel safe because you have *you*.

But in this space you are not even focused on your size. You *know* you are a remarkable human, and you have such a deep appreciation and level of care for yourself that an excess of anything no longer appeals or even appears in your life. When we choose to drink alcohol, we are spitting in the eye of our greatness, dulling ourselves so we feel less, do less, shine less. Sharing a drink over a celebration is a very different scenario from the daily grind of alcohol, and one to be enjoyed if you like to do so. Of course alcohol can be good for your soul. And only you know whether you are nourishing your soul or dimming your light.

You shut down your insight, you shut down your feelings, and you shut down your truth when you rely on alcohol to "relax" in the evenings. What you are actually saying when you drink alcohol in excess is that you can't face your reality. Perhaps you can't face it that you can't bare another moment of baby talk (even though you love your children very much), and that feeling leads you to believe that you are a bad person. So, you drink to "cope" with the crazy 5:00 to 6:00 pm period. Perhaps you drink because you had an affair and, even though you stayed in your original relationship, you are bored with your life. You drink to make the life you chose more bearable. Maybe your daily alcohol intake started when you started a new job, one you didn't really want. And you can't face it that you feel so resentful toward your husband, with whom you once shared a beautiful, intimate marriage, because he bought a business that did not do well financially, forcing you back to work against your will. So you drink each evening with a bitter taste in your mouth, justifying your consumption through your story that you deserve it because you work so bleeping hard. What you actually deserve is to see your own brilliance and then bask in it. You would never want to shut off from that, and alcohol abuse effortlessly exits your life.

Knowing this does not mean that you now have permission to judge yourself every time you want to drink alcohol. If you drink it, enjoy it. I'm not telling you what to do or what not to do. I simply want you to see why you do what you do, especially if what you do is harming you.

If you truly want amazing health that feels effortless, then begin to observe your own behaviors. For example, when you want the alcohol or the food that doesn't serve you, ask yourself what you really want. It might be rest, a hug, or recognition for all you do in a day, or it may be to forget the pain in your heart because someone you love is very ill. All of these things are just pain, emotional pain. And emotional pain will not kill you. In fact, I've learned that quite often it can offer the most magical insight into a part of you that is precious and powerful all at once... often precisely what you are searching for in the food. Imagine realizing that the precious and powerful piece inside you is the most extraordinary best friend you could ever ask to walk beside you through life.

My intention for this book was to show you through science and emotion, and the links between them, that it is always about more than the food. Food is simply a way that we cope. Weight, whether it is too much or too little is a by–product of your coping strategies and a reflection of your beliefs. Excess weight is what happens when you use food to flatten your life.

From this moment on I want you to spend at least five minutes every day recognizing all that you contribute to this world, just by being who you are. And let that recognition light a flame inside you that with every day grows stronger and brighter from the kindness you show yourself through your lifestyle choices and your thoughts. And may that light guide you home to the radiance you have always been.

References and Resources

I have included this section for numerous purposes. First, if you enjoy science there are some fascinating publications listed here. These are written in a scientific reference format. There are also books I've cited in the text, listed in full here if further reading in a particular area interests you.

Due to the overwhelming number of requests I have received for this, I have set up what is called my "Registered Readers" section on my website: www.accidentallyoverweight.com.

Nutrition information is always changing and I am passionate about keeping you up to date with the latest and most insightful aspects of health and well-being. Please be sure to visit my website and register for this free service so you don't miss a thing! This service will also allow you to be informed about my live seminars, as I travel extensively and bring my message to life. It is my favorite thing to do.

After reading *Accidentally Overweight*, you may ask, what's next? I have had so many emails from people all over the world saying they feel like I've read their diary when it comes to describing how they feel in the pages of this book. People tell me they want more of this type of information and a specific program to follow that encompasses guidance with food, hormone balancing, and strategies that give them further insight into their emotional eating patterns. I cannot encourage you enough to check out the array of options on my websites.

My mission is to educate and inspire people and help them change the relationship they have with their bodies and their health and put the power of choice back in their hands. I don't want food to rule anyone anywhere ever.

So visit: www.drlibby.com and www.accidentallyoverweight.com and continue your optimal health journey. It's such an honor to assist you.

Not all of the puzzle pieces have additional resources listed as I have read and studied widely (sometimes from very geeky biochemistry textbooks), and this book is the culmination of my knowledge, experience, observation, and intuition to date.

DIGESTION

Horvath, K., Perman, J.A. (2002), "Autistic disorder and gastrointestinal disease" in *Current Opinions in Pediatrics* 14 (5): 583-7.

Horvath, K., Perman, J.A. (2002) "Autism and gastrointestinal symptoms" in *Current Gastroenterology Reports* 4 (3): 251-8.

Horvath, K., Papadimitriou, J.C. Rabsztyn, A., Drachenberg C., Tildon, J.T. (1999), "Gastrointestinal abnormalities in children with autistic disorders" in *Journal of Pediatrics,* 135 (5): 559-63.

Jin, W., Wang, H., Ji, Y., Hu, Q., Yan, W., Chen, G., Yin, H. (2008), "Increased intestinal inflammatory response and gut barrier dysfunction in Nrf2-deficient mice after traumatic brain injury" 44 (1): 135-40.

SEX HORMONES

Naish, Francesca and Roberts, Janette. *Better Health for Better Babies* series. Sydney: Random House, 1997.

Northrup, Dr Christiane. *Women's Bodies Women's Wisdom.* London: Judy Piatkus Ltd, 1998.

GUT BACTERIA

Gottschall, Elaine. *Breaking the Vicious Cycle*. Baltimore: Kirkton Pr Ltd, 1994 (for the Specific Carbohydrate Diet).

Ley, R.E., Turnbaugh, P.J., Klein, S., Gordon, J.I. (2006), "Microbial ecology: Human gut microbes associated with obesity" in *Nature*, 444 (7122): 1022-1023 (21 December 2006).

THYROID

Coates, Dr Karen and Perry, Vincent. *Embracing the Warrior: An Essential Guide for Women* Burleigh Heads, Arteriol Press, 2007.

INSULIN

Chek, Paul. *How to Eat, Move and Be Healthy!* Encinitas: C.H.E.K Institute LLC, 2004.

Isganaitis, E. and Lustig, R.H. (2005), "Fast Food, Central Nervous System Insulin Resistance, and Obesity" in *Arteriosclerosis Thrombosis Vascular Biology*, 25: 2451-2462.

Lustig, R.H. (2006), "Childhood Obesity: Behavioral aberration or biochemical drive? Reinterpreting the First Law of Thermodynamics" *Nature Clinical Practice, Endocrinology & Metabolism*, Review

2 (8): 447-457.

Lustig, R.H. (2006) "The "Skinny" on Childhood Obesity: How Our Western environment starves kids' brains" in Pediatric Annals, 35 (12): 899-907.

ALKALINITY

Boutenko, Victoria. *The Green Smoothie Revolution*. Berkley: North Atlantic Books, 2009.

EMOTIONS

Epstein, Donny. *The 12 Stages of Healing*. Amber-Allen Publishers. 1994.

Hay, Louise. *You Can Heal Your Life*. Carlsbad: Hay House Inc, 2004.

Robbins, Anthony. *Awaken the Giant Within*. London: Simon & Schuster Ltd, 1992.

Acknowledgements

O f all of the people on earth, I have the privilege of spending my life with the amazing Chris Weaver. Thank you for your passion, your humor, your eyes, your arms, your immense generosity, and for opening me to a new phase of learning and discovery. Thank you for being a guiding light for me and helping me take my messages to the world. You surprise and delight me, and I adore you.

To my dear Mum and Dad. Thank you for the way you raised me and for loving me unconditionally. I am who I am mostly because of you both, and I wouldn't be doing this work without the gifts of my delightful childhood. Mum, thank you for being the kindest lady on the planet and my best friend. Thank you Dad for being the wonderful provider and friend that you have always been to me.

John Aiken, aka J. Dizzle, thank you for sharing the "Accidentally" name with me. John is a psychologist who has written a wonderful book called *Accidentally Single* and when he told me the name, I thought, my gosh! That's gold as my clients are *Accidentally Overweight*. Thanks for sharing and for encouraging me to fly above the radar.

Thank you to a very special place called Gwinganna Lifestyle Retreat in Queensland, Australia, for Her nurturing of me. The land and the passionate, life-loving people that make up this amazing place will always carry a sense of home for me. I am eternally grateful to the process a stay at Gwinganna offers Her guests because it was through this process that I first caught a glimpse of the biochemistry and the psychology of what I now call *Accidentally Overweight*. Big love to Sharon and Karl.

Thank you to Petrea for her belief in me, for the way she encouraged me to get this out there, and for being such fun. You rock!

Thank you to my precious Miss Bliss (hi Bella!) for her magical heart and her unconditional love for me. Thank you! I love you. Thanks to Leisel and Ruby Red Rose for the cutest voicemails ever during the biggest work (mission) year of my life so far and to all of my friends for their patience while I hibernated and wrote my beloved book and spent no time on the phone.

Thanks will always go to Professor Tim Roberts

and Associate Professor Hugh Dunstan for their passion for bugs (gut and infective), steroid hormones, biochemistry, immunology and microbiology, and for the inspiration they offered before and during my PhD to explore the "whys" behind numerous health conditions. And to Dr Merv Garrett for smashing my brain wide open back in 1997 and being the original pioneer. You changed the course of my life and I am forever grateful to you.

Kate Wilkie, thank you for coming into my life. It is such a joy to know you and have you work alongside me, practicing the Dr. Libby method. Thank you, too, to Collette Moss, my amazing assistant who makes it all come together. I'd be lost without you. And thanks to Garry Kewish for his unwavering support and guidance. I am very grateful to you, Garry. And to Caroline, my American editor, thank you for your input and your appreciation of this manuscript. I value your contribution immensely.

Thank you to Tony and Sage Robbins for their gifts of insight into the tremendous heart of real human psychology. Tony, you are a genius, and Sage, your feminine essence is a gift to the world. Massive thanks and recognition to Deborah Battersby for her contribution to the world, most recently in the form of Em-Matrix, and to Deb's co-founder Dr. Sam Hazeldine, who is the embodiment of excitement!

Thank you to Louise Hay for her pioneering work into the meta-physical basis of health conditions. There are times when the lessons I have learned from all of these people have allowed a client to become open to what was really at the heart of their health challenge. As I love to say, it is never about the food. And yet it *is* about the food for that is some people's doorway to their own magnificence. And thanks be to God. You are so gracious and so great!

Thank you to the children with autism who, through my work with them and their families, gave me an insight into far more than just gut function and poop! Like canaries in the mines, these children are gifts who offer us a warning that we cannot continue living the way that we are. Our world is too toxic for them. And the *Accidentally Overweight* are but just one more sign of this.

To everyone who knows somewhere inside of them that it is not about the food, I hope you have just been reminded of what you already know.

About Dr Libby

Born and educated in Australia, Dr Libby Weaver (PhD) studied at the University of Newcastle from 1993 until 2006. She completed a Bachelor of Health Science (Nutritional and Dietetics) with Honors in 1998 and went on to complete a PhD in the biochemical and nutritional factors affecting children with autism. Through this work Libby came to better understand and communicate the relationships between the food we eat, our thoughts and beliefs, and the way our body then expands or shrinks.

Since 1999, Dr Libby has been working with individual patients from all walks of life, from stay-at-home mums to Hollywood stars. She set up and ran an organic café and she has been an integral person in the creation of two of Australia's major health retreats where she not only designed the nutritional philosophies, but also performed the role of Program Director.

Dr Libby moved to New Zealand in 2007 to be with her husband Chris, since which time they have created a Holistic Nutrition Consultancy that provides people all over the world with consultations as well as empowering, informative seminars and retreats. Dr Libby is a regular columnist for many magazines including *Next, Good Health and Taste*, and she is a passionate and sought after international keynote speaker.

www.drlibby.com

www.accidentallyoverweight.com